Alan Greenberg

LOVE IN VAIN

A Vision of Robert Johnson

New foreword by Martin Scorsese
Introduction by Stanley Crouch

DA CAPO PRESS • NEW YORK

Library of Congress Cataloging in Publication Data

Greenberg, Alan.
    Love in vain: a vision of Robert Johnson / Alan Greenberg.—1st Da Capo
Press ed. 1994
    p.   cm.
    Originally published: Garden City, N.Y.: Doubleday, 1983.
    Discography: p.
    ISBN 0-306-80557-X
    1. Johnson, Robert, d. 1938. 2. Blues musicians—Mississippi—Biography.
I. Title.
ML420.J735G7 1994   93-48052
782.42164′3′092—dc20   CIP
                                                                      MN

Acknowledgements

PREACHIN' BLUES, WALKIN' BLUES, SWEET HOME CHICAGO, RAMBLIN' ON MY
MIND, TRAVELING RIVERSIDE BLUES, IF I HAD POSSESSION OVER JUDGMENT
DAY, COME ON IN MY KITCHEN, I BELIEVE I'LL DUST MY BROOM, KIND
HEARTED WOMAN BLUES, WHEN YOU GOT A GOOD FRIEND, CROSS ROAD
BLUES, LITTLE QUEEN OF SPADES, FROM FOUR UNTIL LATE, STOP BREAKIN'
DOWN BLUES, MILK COW'S CALF BLUES, PHONOGRAPH BLUES, 32-20 BLUES,
Words and Music by Robert Johnson
Copyright © 1978 King of Spades Music
All Rights Reserved Used by Permission

STORMY WEATHER, Lyrics by Ted Koehler, Music by Harold Arlen
© 1933 Mills Music, Inc. © Renewed 1961 Arko Music Corp.
International Copyright Secured All Rights Reserved Used by Permission

COOL DRINK OF WATER BLUES, Words and Music by Tommy Johnson
Copyright 1929 Peer International Corporation
Copyright Renewed All Rights Reserved Used by Permission

CANNED HEAT BLUES, Words and Music by Tommy Johnson
Copyright 1930 Peer International Corporation
Copyright Renewed All Rights Reserved Used by Permission

First Da Capo Press edition 1994

This Da Capo Press paperback edition of *Love in Vain* is an unabridged republication of the
edition published in Garden City, New York in 1983, with author emendations, and with the
addition of a new foreword by Martin Scorsese and new illustrations. It is reprinted by
arrangement with Alan Greenberg.

Copyright © 1983 by Alan Greenberg
Foreword copyright © 1994 by Martin Scorsese

Published by Da Capo Press, Inc.
A Subsidiary of Plenum Publishing Corporation
233 Spring Street, New York, N.Y. 10013

All Rights Reserved

Manufactured in the United States of America

Contents

Foreword

I remember first hearing about Robert Johnson at a time when all my friends who were serious about music seemed to be listening to the blues—the *real* stuff—guys like Blind Lemon Jefferson, Lightnin' Hopkins, Howlin' Wolf, Elmore James, B. B. King, and Muddy Waters. Of them all, Johnson was the most intriguing—perhaps because he was also the most obscure. The thing about Robert Johnson was that he only existed on his records. He was pure legend. Even the experts didn't have much of a clue as to who he really was; just that he recorded a total of 29 songs, that he died young, and that he was the greatest Delta bluesman of all time. I think it was the combination of all these blues masterpieces and the complete absence of hard facts—the absolute mystery and the indisputable genius—that for me charged the Johnson legend with an irresistible appeal and attracted me to Alan Greenberg's remarkable screenplay.

With this issue of a second edition, it seems to me even more appropriate that *Love in Vain*, though as yet unproduced, should be published in book form. For me the script reads like literature. Alan's unique style captures the Mississippi Delta in images of stark sensuality and a matter-of-fact pain and poverty that are the very essence of Johnson's music. In its mix of Depression Era realism with Southern black folklore, I see the script less as a literal history than as a spiritual biography. Johnson is like some haunted prophet who must go into the desert to find his voice, and who plays his music not out of choice but because he has no choice; he has become possessed by the spirit of the blues.

That the script represents this possession as a literal pact with the devil—this was the legend of Johnson's extraordinary guitar skill—only speaks to the existential predicament of all artists—and one of the cruel paradoxes of human nature—that our finest art is born from the wellspring of pain.

—MARTIN SCORSESE
New York City, 1993

Introduction

Printing the Legend

> "This is the West, sir. When the
> legend becomes fact, print the legend."
>
> —John Ford, "The Man Who Shot
> Liberty Valance"

I find it fitting that the first book written about Mississippi's
Delta blues genius Robert Johnson is grounded as much in
myth, legend and tall tale as in research. The work's obvious
inclination toward the fantastic and the cultural metaphors of su-
perstition separates it from those largely fictional film biogra-
phies which are pushed forward as factual; it also proposes that
we can learn as much from good mythology as from fine documentation—if the mythology carries or transmits how a world
may have *felt* to those participants, onlookers and descendants
swept up in the lore of time and impatient with flat facts. The vision of LOVE IN VAIN, then, swells personality, circumstance and
action to the proportions of legend and propels that legend with
such audacity and awe, humor and terror, sensuality and dread-
laden sorrow that it is obvious how much the writer has been
touched and inspired by the broad and mysterious passions of
Robert Johnson's life and music.

Alan Greenberg's Robert Johnson is as much an American bard

as the anonymous cowboys of the last century who created both Pecos Bill and the songs that filled the long nights under the big skies. This Robert Johnson appears as a figure we recognize yet find vastly mysterious. The consternation and outrage he inspires in the boyfriends of the local girls he charms through his exotic powers as drifting musician fall roughly into a familiar cinematic key. But he is mysterious because his gifts float his life and his art across the threshold of genius, where the beautiful can be as interwoven with the violent, the bloody, the courageous and the painful, as is childbirth. That his music can inspire or instigate contradictory passions and actions as far removed as love and murder—or appear to—adds to the mysterious, even dangerous qualities of the stranger this Robert Johnson remains throughout the work.

Yet Johnson's world also remains strange to the character himself, and it is a place in which he is no more comfortable by the end of his life than he was when we first met him. It is a universe made so cockeyed by constant drinking that reality is a series of dulled, sullenly received or exuberantly pursued experiences. Much like a jungle, that jook-joint area of life contains the lovely and the predatory, most of them inebriated and stumbling into each other as love and violence bump and grind in a sweaty and impoverished half-light. Robert Johnson's delicate relationship to it all makes him a tragic character, for the essence of the tragic flaw is that it dooms by throwing the hero out of step with the world. The human significance of the tragic hero is measured by the nature of the character's emotional response to the situation. Robert Johnson's response was to narrate through the vehicle of music the dimensions of a sensibility both wooed and repulsed, appreciated and brutalized by a nightmare world.

The nature of Robert Johnson's nightmare, however, is much larger and more primal than the tools of sociology would allow us to explicate, for then we would only be led down the purple path of accusations based on economic and environmental shortcomings. All of those accusations are true, but they are not true enough to say more to us about the human condition than Johnson's art of the blues, which is a music that shakes its fist at fate as often as it accepts the saddening upshots of bad decisions and bad luck. For the blues sensibility, the constant riddle is that of human joy and human dissatisfaction, and what the two have to do with human conduct. Yet because the erotic is seen through the blues in a broad and unsentimental fashion, its morality is far from stilted and very complex, with neither man nor woman the more driven or given to shady actions because of sexual desires. Consequently, the blues gives an epic sense of the erotic to American music and tears the cotton candy shroud from the boudoir, speaking of the elegant and the raw, the ennobling and the debilitating—all pushed down the listener's consciousness with often bittersweet and sardonic images. Only through an awareness of these things can we approach the nightmare of Robert Johnson with firmer footing than the sociological statistic.

The mythological is as firm a footing as any. The dilemma Alan Greenberg faced in creating his Robert Johnson was awesome because it called for depicting a man of genius who was also an intuitive artist and a product of a rough-and-tumble world not far removed from the disorder of cattle towns on cowboy weekends, logging camps or the communities that grew up in the shadows of gold strikes. Johnson's aesthetic cartography made use of spirits and demons, images from the industrial world and from the marketplace, vulgar threats and dares from the hangouts of corner boys and thugs, all interlaced with phrases and themes passed on to him from his predecessors. The result was a vision as domestically surreal as tall tales or the "dozens." In fact, one could easily say that Robert Johnson shaped an art in which the tallest tales of human experience, whether wonderful or woeful, were equaled by a craftsmanship and imagination that elevated his work from the amorphous world of Delta Ned Buntlines to that of fish stories lining up to march on the universe of *Moby Dick*. His genius was that of the innovator: Johnson expanded the possibilities of his idiom through the creation and delivery of his lyrics and the rudely or tenderly beautiful gradations of his guitar playing. Like another domestic pioneer, Daniel Boone, his victories against the wilderness led to legends.

The segregated Southern society in which Robert Johnson developed contained, for all its Jim Crow laws, a kind of black frontier world that came into existence after nightfall. There black men and women could act as wildly as they wished as long as they didn't harm the lives or ownings of whites. Where the blues was invented, refined and danced to, people who usually did hard, mindless and boring work in cotton fields, sawmills, on turpentine farms and so on put on the dog. Just as the verbal imagination and legendary feats espoused by frontiersmen and cowboys were responses to harsh, impersonal difficulties, the jook-joint culture was also one of homemade glamor and glory. There black people dressed up, they strutted, they drank, they swore, they told tall tales and boasted; they also gambled and flirted, since money and flesh could be fast, loose and recklessly used. Where Davy Crockett exemplified the frontier vision when he boasted, "I can walk like an ox, run like a fox, swim like an eel, yell like an Indian, fight like a devil, spout like an earthquake, make love like a mad bull, and swallow a nigger whole without choking if you butter his head and pin his ears back," Rudy Ray Moore recites the black equivalent when he says, "I was born in a barrel of butcher knives, I been shot in my ass with two Colt .45s, I been bit by a shark and stung by an eel, I chew up railroad iron and spit out steel." Bluesman Peetie Wheatstraw called himself "the Devil's son-in-law" and "the high sheriff of Hell." In one song, Robert Johnson chants, "I'm going to upset your backbone, put your kidneys to sleep, do the breakaway on your liver, and dare your heart to beat!"

The development of the blues itself parallels the evolution of popular nineteenth-century characters and forms like minstrelsy; both were responses to the growing feeling of group identity among lower-class rural whites who had come to the cities and wanted art that addressed their experience through dramatic parable, monologue, melodrama, satire or skit. In the backwoods of the Delta blues, the art could be crude, even rude, but it wasn't to be pretentious or given to sentimentality, probably a secular version of the attitude that had led slaves to strip flowery language and notes from the Christian hymns when they learned them. It is possible that the rough texture of life could only be countered by religious or secular art forged with the spirit of steel, not the tin of the maudlin. The inner workings of human lives were at issue and, as Albert Murray says in *Stomping the Blues*, ". . . the spirit, after all, is not only what is threatened but is also the very part of you that is assumed to be the most vulnerable. For what is ultimately at stake is morale, which is to say the will to persevere, the disposition to persist and perhaps prevail; and what must be avoided by all means is a failure of nerve." So blues became a narration and an interpretation of experience, a music of courtship and battle cries that was performed for demanding and often dangerous audiences, or audiences that frequently included violent and dangerous men and women.

Even though he was the king of this rough-and-tumble carnival, the bluesman was not above danger, and those dangers he faced had much to do with what he provided on one hand and represented on another. The bluesman supplied the musical background against which hearts were won or broken; he was the unknown drifter, or the notorious one. He could raise the dance and erotic fevers of his listeners and express, in however limited a way, another level of sophistication than that of the ordinary workingman at the jook joint trying to have a good time. A traveler, he sometimes came to town with new slang, predicted in his dress future fashion, and dazzled the girls, many of whom were primed for almost anything that suggested excitement beyond what little they'd come to expect from everyday life. At the height of the evening, a familiar man had the chance to be moved by and abandoned for the music-making stranger. If the girl was the wrong one, the bluesman could feel physical wrath from the girl herself, a boyfriend, a relative. The balance was always a proverbially delicate one.

LOVE IN VAIN shapes its tale around the problems of balance and, in the rendering of Robert Johnson's drives and adventures, gives us a vision as elemental and subtle as that of a fine Western. Its themes and struggles come together as a tall-tale nightmare tragedy filled with aesthetic gunfights, camaraderie, raw or melodramatic romance, comic characters, satire and figures that prove out the slave hymn adage, "Old Satan is a liar and a conjuror, too; if you don't mind, he'll conjure you." But in this case the ambitious young man doesn't desire the position of top gun, biggest rancher, best horseman or such, he wants to be the best Delta blues musician. The introduction of a Faustian element connects perfectly to the black folk belief that the blues was the Devil's music and its practitioners hellbound. It also suggests, in perfect mythic keeping, that supreme creation can be some sort of a challenge to the gods and can result from a pact with dark forces. Before Johnson reaches the tragic consequences of his deal, we are given many images of darkness, or night, as the liberating province of tender desires, genial celebration and the savage moods of the destructive. The writer does a fine job of showing Johnson's personality slowly dissolve as the character of his music becomes more distinctive and innovative, as if the art came to replace a soul thrown bloody lump by bloody lump onto the fiery breast of the Devil.

Stanley Crouch

Dedicated to the memory of my father,
Howard Roosevelt Greenberg

When I leave this town
I'm gonna bid you fair farewell,
And when I return again you'll have
A great long story to tell.

Love In Vain

1. EXTERIOR. COTTON FIELD AND CHURCH. NIGHT.

A hard rain, and the tiny white clapboard church on the edge of the field glows softly by candlelight from within. There, an entranced choir of female voices coos and moans hypnotically.

A stout black woman is seen stepping out the back door of the church and into the downpour. She picks up an ax beneath the chinaberry tree and starts hustling about, chopping determinedly at the rain and the muddy ground. From inside the church, the voice of the PREACHER rises above his choir.

PREACHER (off)

Brothers and sisters, in being a duty-bound servant of God I stand before you tonight to try to bring you a message of "Thus sayeth the Lord." Seems I'm hoarse some now with the cold, but if you'll stick by me a little while and God is willing we will preach. The hounds of hell are so fast on our trail that we've got to go sometime whether we like it or not. So here we are tonight, to hear what the spirit has to say. . . .

The rain subsides; the stout woman stops her chopping under the tree and re-enters the church.

SUPER: "The Mississippi Delta, near Robinsonville, 1930"

2. EXTERIOR. GRAVEL ROAD. NIGHT.

One last rumble of thunder leaves a wet and ghostly stillness. From far down the road comes a glimmering of headlights; we hear the sputtering strain of an old automobile, and the mud. When the jalopy finally lumbers into view it stalls. Two aged black sharecroppers get out and stagger to the front of the car.

Chewing on a wad of tobacco, the DRIVER checks beneath the hood. His back to the camera to the driver's rear, the PASSENGER urinates onto the roadside while telling a story.

> PASSENGER
>
> . . . when they was out in the field workin'. Overseer he say they ain't much good, gonna tie 'em up and whip 'em. But they say, "Mr. Overseer, you ain't gonna lick me," and runs to the river. Overseer he sure thought he catch 'em when they get there, only 'fore he get to 'em they rise up in the air and fly away. Fly right back to Africa. Yessuh. I reckon that was yonder past Friars Point—

> DRIVER

Le's push.

The driver spits out a jawful of black tobacco juice as they head for the rear of the car. Here we notice a long bundle strapped across the trunk: the dead body of a young black man.

A haunting music descends from the clouds. It is a remarkable wordless chant, a soft lament with guitar entitled "Dark Was the Night, Cold Was the Ground," recorded in 1927 by Blind Willie Johnson. The two skinny men push the jalopy up the road as other people begin to filter onto the road from the fields. The sharecroppers glance at the car and body tied behind while proceeding oppositely. The camera slowly follows. The music continues as the titles appear.

SUPER: "LOVE IN VAIN"

The anonymous figures trek onward, then step off the road toward the middle of a grim cotton field where a strange shack made of rusted sheet metal stands. The dilapidated place sparkles in the distance from the rich amber light of dampered kerosene lamps inside. Surrounding the shack, bottle lamps with rope wicks flicker, throwing angry shadows off the trees with sagging limbs.

The camera creeps closer as the music starts to fade. The joint is jammed with sharecroppers. There is feverish dancing inside and out.

FADE TO BLACK.

3. INTERIOR. JOOK JOINT. NIGHT.

Images of chaos, of rough black bodies rubbing and sweating and dancing wildly in the heated kerosene haze, powered by a loud pounding rhythm raging with erotic dread. Walls painted randomly in different dark shades close in on the strange scene. People are half seen, acts are half followed, as in dreams.

Seated on a chair amid the tumult, a muscular young man named WILLIE BROWN frantically ties a broken string on his giant guitar. In the corner, his partner SON HOUSE fends off a woman who keeps pouring beer into his steel guitar. He guzzles the beer out of his guitar until it is dry, as Willie yells to him.

4

WILLIE

Son, take over! Hey Son, take over now quick!

The furious momentum increases even without the music. Son rushes toward Willie as his female admirer gulps down the rest of her beer. Picking up on the sizzling tempo by stomping his foot and sliding a jagged glass bottleneck over the guitar strings, Son explodes with improvised song.

SON (singing)

"No use hollerin', no use screamin' and cryin'./ You know you got a home, mama, long as I got mine!"

Willie finally knots his string and trades verses with Son, shouting the song out with all his might.

WILLIE (singing)

"I start' to kill my woman till she lay down 'cross the bed./ She looked so ambitious I took back everything I said!"

The air is ecstatically wicked. The intense activity is a cross between contemporary-style dance and heavy petting. One woman struts like a chicken as her mate makes a face like a fish. Others pound the walls. One guy grabs onto a window and jerks it off its hinges. The surging music ensues.

4. EXTERIOR. JOOK JOINT. NIGHT.

A local bootlegger's makeshift bar is crowded by patrons of the jook. ROBERT JOHNSON, a slender nineteen-year-old neatly dressed in striped pants with suspenders, a clean white shirt and two-toned wing-tip shoes, watches as the bootlegger fills his soda bottle with hootch.

Robert walks beneath a tree to the edge of the yard. He empties his bottle in three or four turns, then he stares fixedly upon the immense whispering field. In a few seconds he heads back toward the hootch stand.

A lanky, mustachioed youth named GOAT marches into the yard towing his pretty but lame girlfriend LAVENDAR in a wooden wagon. Lavendar beckons Goat as they pass the hootch stand.

LAVENDAR

Say Babyface . . . oh Goat—

GOAT

Don't got the change.

LAVENDAR

What do you got.

GOAT

You, babe.

Goat parks the wagon near Robert's vacated spot beneath the tree. Lavendar remains standing in the wagon.

GOAT

Be right back.

LAVENDAR

You gonna jook some, Goat? That ain't fair since I got this leg.

GOAT

Quiet now, Lavendar. Just gonna fix us up some shoeshine. I be right back.

LAVENDAR

You gonna dance in there, I know it—ain't you,
Goat? Ain't you, Babyface? Say Goat—

Goat turns toward the shack, ignoring Lavendar, who
takes to shouting out a popular blues. Robert returns
with a full bottle of corn liquor to resume his drunken
vigil.

LAVENDAR (singing)

"I say jake leg jake leg jake leg jake leg,/ Tell
me what in the world you gonna do—"

Lavendar performs live atop her wooden wagon, bellowing and writhing. Robert continues his serious drinking,
oblivious to Lavendar. His steady deep-set eyes, now
glazed, reflect a precarious inner resolve.

Lavendar spots Robert and eyes the handsome youth
over.

LAVENDAR (singing)

"Mama mama mama mama cried out and said,
'Oh, Lord,/ Ain't there somethin' in the world
poor daddy can do. . . .'"

She stops singing. Still examining Robert, she rests her
stiff leg over the edge of the wagon and puts her hand
on her hip. A strap on her threadbare red dress slips off
her shoulder. Robert ignores her.

LAVENDAR

Where's that Goat? Where's my Hooky Doodle?
Motherin' sonofabitch. In there jookin' with
them free-fuckin' whores givin' out pussy they
can't even sell. I'll kill him. That Goat he got a

cock so long they gonna jack him off to let the coffin lid down.

Say, Robert Johnson, now isn't that so? Say, Robert Johnson, how 'bout you?

Robert swigs some hootch and gazes upon the field.

LAVENDAR

Huh? Ain't that you, Robert Johnson? Good-boy Robert Dusty? Good-boy Robert Dusty never seen his papa's face? You come here Rusty Dusty an' tote Lavendar to Hooky Doodle's door over yonder.

Robert, perturbed, ignores Lavendar while finishing off his hootch. He holds the empty bottle and stares.

LAVENDAR

Hmmm. A bastard. You a bastard if there ever was one, Robert Johnson. You never seen his true face 'cause I know you never seen him. Your papa's name was Noah. Your mama, huh, she mightn't've married no Noah, an' that's a fact, but sweet Julia and ol' Noah musta done something *bad* 'cause there you are. Say, Robert Johnson, there you *are*.

Robert walks over and faces Lavendar.

ROBERT

You tote yourself.

LAVENDAR (softly)

Set you on fire, Robert—

Robert tosses his bottle aside and walks toward the jook.

LAVENDAR

Lavendar better find ol' Goat herself.

As Robert enters the side door to the jook, Lavendar limps after him, towing her wooden wagon. Upon reaching the side door she parks the wagon and, quickly, steps into it and stands alone, as before.

5. INTERIOR. JOOK KITCHEN AREA. NIGHT.

A tight alcove filled by three women and Goat. The women are dipping snuff and drinking. Goat, a grotesque hare's foot strung around his neck, pours a can labeled "Shoe Shine" through a slice of bread into a tin cup, filtering the liquid polish clear.

A WOMAN with sinking eyelids clutches onto Goat as he tastes his brew, then grins beatifically. Robert pushes through as Goat balances two overflowing cups, heading for the door.

LAVENDAR (off)

"Jake leg jake leg jake leg jake leg—" What the hell's goin' on!

WOMAN

Aw, Goat, you keep givin' her that shoeshine stuff'll kill her someday—an' I be here waitin'! Mmm, come to mama—

6. INTERIOR. JOOK JOINT. NIGHT.

Bedlam reigns as Willie and Son keep playing. Willie spots Robert by the door and frowns. Tapping his brow with a clean white cloth that glows in the darkening amber, Robert's eyes are fixed upon the musicians.

WILLIE (singing)

"Jinx all 'round, jinx all 'round my bed./ Got up
this mornin' and it likened to kill me dead—"

As Robert moves into the crowd, a burly man lifts a sexy
wench onto a table. Someone lights a candle and sets it
upright between her feet as she dances.

Robert sits on the floor at the musicians' feet. As Robert
studies Willie's hands, Willie glares back.

WILLIE (sternly)

What's it say, Little Robert?

The wench squats and flirts with the flame as aroused
male voices shout encouragement.

WILLIE

What's it say, Little Robert? You hear it?
Where's your harp?

ROBERT

I don't blow no harp.

WILLIE

Where's your harp at?

ROBERT

Playin' gui-tar now.

SON (singing)

"Blues ain't nothin' but a low-down shakin'
chill./ If you ain't had 'em, honey, hope you
never will—"

His hands cupped over his mouth, Robert suddenly lets go with a brilliant, biting wail on his harmonica.

Son's left hand streaks across the guitar neck. We see it bleeding badly from a cut from the jagged glass bottleneck. He keeps playing.

In one abrupt swoop the wench dips down and picks up the burning candle between her legs. The jook erupts in cheers.

WILLIE

What's it say, Robert—can't you tell? Ain't you sayin'?

Son's female admirer pours hootch on his bleeding hand. With a yelp he leaps to his feet and pushes his way out as the wench tries a rolled dollar bill.

Robert stares at Son's fallen guitar, his white shirt spotted with blood. Willie glares at Robert, plucks a string hard and snaps it. Robert instantly pounces on Son's guitar and sits with it facing the wall.

WILLIE (off)

Dammit, Robert, put that down!

In the eye of the pounding storm all around him, Robert cradles the steel guitar tensely, struggling with it, squeezing it to produce sound. Willie lunges at him clumsily; Robert ducks away and, now hooting and hollering madly, he starts swinging the guitar over his head.

Son rushes back to see his guitar flying. The first punches are thrown. Robert crawls across the floor and reaches for the kerosene lamp.

7. EXTERIOR. GRAVEL ROAD. NIGHT.

We see the lights go out inside the jook from afar. Perched atop her wagon under the only burning lamp, Lavendar exults in the night.

LAVENDAR

Whoa, California! He's blowed it up with that stuff! He's blowed it up!

8. EXTERIOR. COTTON FIELD. MIDNIGHT.

Leaving the noisy jook behind, Son and Willie trek home through the high stalks.

WILLIE

Sure am glad Charley showed.

SON

But you catch that decoration? Clown's got a lick so dizzy take a three-legged man to dance to it.

WILLIE

He's a great man, that Charley Patton, he's a great big man—

SON

Hushhh . . .

Robert is kneeling on the ground amid the stalks, bent over, near tears.

Son and Willie stand quietly over Robert's shoulder.

WILLIE

Black nigger baby gonna take care of hisself.

Gently they lift Robert up by his arms. Robert slips his
white kerchief into a pocket and brushes off, eyeing the
full moon.

ROBERT

Moon almost full now—

From high overhead, an aerial view of the livid shifting
clouds above the horizon and the slumbering fields
below. Three tiny figures inch along toward shacks a
few fields away.

SON (off)

Robert, you all right. Don't you think so Willie
Brown. You just do your best 'cause there ain't
no better place to do your best than right here
in the U. S. of A. Work hard, even here in Mississippi, you get whatever it is you want. Same
over in Arkansas, Lou'siana and Memphis.

WILLIE (off)

Best stay 'way from Alabama though. Lotsa
dead folk. Act like heathens down there—folks
stomp all over you.

SON (off)

That's right—just do your best. Don't say nothin'
'bout nobody. Stay the place you're in, where
you're told. Get down on yourself, forget it
'cause remember now, this is a free enterprise
system we got here. . . .

FADE OUT.

9. EXTERIOR. MISSISSIPPI RIVER. MORNING.

The great river is visible in a soft blue curving sweep. In the distance, through the mist, we see an old riverboat coming from the bend. Its decks are laden with tall stacks of cotton bales.

Drifting in with the boat, the atmospheric sound of sharecroppers chanting slowly in the nearby fields. The hypnotic song is sung not in chorus but as a swelling up of harmonizing solos. The melody ranges from a minor note of despair to a triumphant major.

FIELD SINGERS (off)

"Captain, I due to be in Monroe, Lou'siana,/ Ohhhhhh in them long, hot summer days—"

10. EXTERIOR. COTTON FIELDS. MORNING.

A vast whiteness of cotton over a sea of green, with the scattered figures of black workers moving against it in bold relief. The stark cadence of voices continues. The sunlight is blinding.

FIELD SINGERS

"Black gal, if I never more see you,/ Ohhhhhhhhhh in them long, hot summer days—"

Individual men, women and children toil in the awful heat. They stoop before the plants, pull the white seedy cotton from the bolls and place it in long white sacks trailing behind them. The movements are graceful and rhythmic; the workers are entranced so to cope.

We see Goat across the field atop a billowing cloud of picked cotton in the mule-drawn wooden wagon. He hollers out a song while strumming hard on his old guitar. Closer in, HENRY SIMS bends low to pick apart a testy boll. He steps back so T-BONE can chop it with his hoe.

Robert stares blankly at his hoe as it attacks a boll. The itinerant country preacher ELDER HADLEY shouts out his endless prayers and sermons from the edge of the field, fifty yards away.

ELDER HADLEY

O Lord Almighty beloved Father, again we pray here 'neath Your high fields of mercy, bowed down at Your footstool so to thank You for these earthly lives. And Lord, for hearin' the sinner man's cries. We thank You for gettin' us Your childrens up this mornin' clothed in our right minds—

Robert, perspiring heavily, deep-set eyes staring down at his hoe, chops and chops as the preacher proceeds.

A white pickup truck turns onto the gravel road rimming the field and slowly approaches the preacher.

ELDER HADLEY (off)

—and for seein' through Your holy eyes. O God our Captain King, tuck my ol' soul away in its snow-white chariot and take it way over yonder where they got the Third Heaven, where my sorrows of this world gonna end. Please give to us a restin' place so we can praise Thy name forever, my prayer for Jesus my Redeemer's sake, forever thank God and amen.

The pickup stops. Two pudgy white men, the red-haired FOREMAN with a pistol on his hip and the pinkish, balding HENRY SPEIR, get out and head for the preacher, who has not noticed them.

ELDER HADLEY

My brothers and my sisters, my subject for this mornin' is, "The World Is in a Hell of a Fix"—I mean *this* world's in a hell of a fix! These are dyin' days! These are perilous times! We are living in times of the Businessman! And the Racketeer! And the Bootlegger! And the False Pretender! Men have turned their backs on God!

The foreman interrupts.

FOREMAN

Say, Bishop—

ELDER HADLEY

God is calling! God is calling! The world is upside down!

FOREMAN

Say, Preacher, say, Preach, whoa—let's cut that stuff out now so's we can be of some use, help me find that no-good yodelin' overseer of mine. You seen Goat? Mr. Speir here from town's got some business to see him on.

The preacher eyes Goat, still singing atop his wagon across the field. He shifts his eyes and plays dumb.

ELDER HADLEY (off)

Goat, you said?

FOREMAN (off)

Goat. Bubber Rubberdick.

ELDER HADLEY

Sure is a strange name for a Christian. You got
me, Mr. Foreman. Lord knows where he is.

SPEIR

There, over yonder, I see him— Hey, Goat!
Yahoo! Say, Bubber!

FOREMAN

Leave it to me, Speir—I'm the specialist in nigger nature 'round here.
(hollering)
Hey yahoo Goat! Say Bubber!

The foreman trots out toward the distant wagon.

11. EXTERIOR. COTTON WAGON. MORNING.

Goat stands in the mass of cotton bolls, playing his guitar, singing and hollering in falsetto with abandon.
Looking into the wagon now, we can behold Lavendar
writhing spread-eagled in the whiteness.

GOAT (singing)

"I . . . asked for water, and she give me . . .
gas-o-line,/ Cryin', Lord, Lordy Lord—"

FOREMAN (off)

Say, Goat!

GOAT (startled)

God dog, it's the foreman—

Goat stops singing. In his panic he looks to Lavendar.

LAVENDAR

Piss on 'im, Goat—go on an' git 'im, you can do
it, just don't think 'bout it, crack 'im now, kick
'im, go 'head—

GOAT

Better do somethin' quick.

FOREMAN (off)

Down, Goat! Say down a minute now!

LAVENDAR

Boy, you kick 'im till your shoes are shitty!

Goat gets rid of the guitar by dropping it over the far
side of the wagon. He hops off the back and lopes toward the foreman as Lavendar urges him on in song.

LAVENDAR (singing)

"You got to move, you got to move,/ You got to
move, chile, you got to move—"

Goat's guitar has fallen beside a front wheel of the
wooden wagon. The mule eyes the guitar, then puts its
foot through it and laughs.

LAVENDAR (off)

"But when the Lord get ready/ You got to
move—"

12. EXTERIOR. COTTON FIELD. MORNING.

The foreman and Goat walk peaceably across the field.

FOREMAN

This fella Speir from town's got some record business to talk over, probably wants you to go make him another hit somewheres.

GOAT

Record? Excuse me, sir, but I can't make none of them records no more—I went and sold away my rights. It was a bad deal, Mr. Foreman. I was drinkin' that denature an' was on the kerosene when the Victor man come, an' what he wanted was my rights. So I sold 'em.

FOREMAN

You signed a contract with the Victor Company?

GOAT

Got me six bucks. Cash. Had a pretty song to sing, too. But yessir, I sold 'em my rights.

13. EXTERIOR. COTTON FIELD. AFTERNOON.

Robert chops with his hoe as he has all day beneath the fiery sun. Standing at the edge of the field, the preacher rants incessantly.

His wet face shining with sweat, Robert seems to wince with every word.

ELDER HADLEY (off)

GOD IS CALLING! GOD IS CALLING! My brothers and sisters, there's HARD TIMES that we're having in this world! There's MILLIONS out of work! There's worldwide DEPRESSION! And that is because, this ol' WORLD's in a HELL of a FIX! AND YOU BETTER GET RIGHT WITH GOD!

Lavendar, asleep in the cotton cloud behind Robert, awakens. She rubs her eyes, then she buttons up her blouse and looks around.

ELDER HADLEY (off)

You better get RIGHT, my childrens, because Jesus is RISING! Jesus is RISING!

LAVENDAR (softly)

Goat's gone.

Robert chops and chops obliviously. Over his shoulder we see Lavendar arise, stiff leg extended, atop the white mound fifty yards away.

ELDER HADLEY (off)

GET RIGHT WITH GOD! GET RIGHT WITH GOD!

LAVENDAR

CHRIST'S SAKE ROBERT DUSTY GOAT'S GONE!

ELDER HADLEY (off)

These are the LAST DAYS! These are them LYIN' CRYIN' TIMES when men DESIRE MORE PLEASURE THAN THEY DO MORE GOOD!

LAVENDAR

THEY GOT 'IM ROBERT DUSTY AN' HE'S GONE! OH LORD I HATES TO PONDER SOME FAT-BREASTED BITCH THAT'S SNORIN' IN MY HOOKY DOODLE'S FACE!

Robert chops and chops hypnotically as the voices overhead clash and converge. He never looks at either Lavendar or Elder Hadley.

ELDER HADLEY (off)

YOU GOT TO ATONE! SINNERS! YOU GOT TO ATONE!
OH THEM BULL COWS COULDN'T DO IT! OH THEM
HEIFERS AN' THE BLACK-BLOODED DOVES COULDN'T
DO IT!

LAVENDAR (off)

YOU GONNA COME HERE, DUSTY, SEE YO' POOR
CHERRY RED? YOU GONNA COME OUT HERE TO
THESE HIGH FIELDS? THESE ARE THE HIGH FIELDS,
DUSTY! THESE ARE THE HIGH FIELDS!

In the distance, the camera spies a young mule being
led from the field by a hand. Some crows fly by.

ELDER HADLEY (off)

BUT WAY UP IN HEAVEN FOR A THOUSAND AND
THOUSANDS OF YEARS, THE SON WAS SAYIN' TO THE
FATHER, "PUT UP A SOUL! PUT UP A SOUL!
PREPARE ME A BODY! AN' I'LL GO DOWN AN' MEET
JUSTICE ON OL' CALVARY'S BROW!"

Under a tree a woman unbridles the mule. It struggles
with the woman as she removes the heavy leather straps.

LAVENDAR (off)

SAY SOMETHIN', DUSTY! MY NERVES IS BAD! MY
NERVES IS BAD 'CAUSE I AIN'T DRINKIN' SO MUCH
BUT DUSTY, YOU IS SIN-SICK! YOU IS SIN-SICK AN'
WON'T EVEN SIGNIFY!

The young mule breaks away, knocking the woman
down. It lopes into a far field, trotting about aimlessly.

LAVENDAR (off)

THESE ARE THE HIGH FIELDS, DUSTY!

ELDER HADLEY (off)

OHHH-OOO-OHHHHH! I SEED THE SUN WHEN SHE TURNED HERSELF BLACK AS THE NIGHT! I SEED THE MOON WEEP AN' THE STARS A-FALLIN' FROM THE SKY! OH, AN' THE SAINTS ARE SINGIN' AN' THE LORD'S CRYIN' OUT TO TESTIFY!

LAVENDAR (off)

THESE ARE THE HIGH FIELDS, DUSTY! THESE ARE THE HIGH FIELDS!—

A puff of white smoke in the far field, and the pop of a gun. The young mule twists upward and drops.

LAVENDAR (off)

ROBERT JOHNSON YOU A COWARD!

14. EXTERIOR. COTTON FIELD. TWILIGHT.

Robert suddenly turns about and chops down hard with his hoe, as a cottonmouth snake writhes in the dirt, cut in two. He jerks his soiled head up. The fields are hushed. Far away, the wagon leaves with its mass of cotton as the dinner bell tolls. Lavendar is gone.

Robert rubs his eyes.

Lying dormant in the space vacated by the wagon, Goat's broken guitar remains.

15. EXTERIOR. COTTON FIELD PERIPHERY. TWILIGHT.

Robert trudges off the field with his hoe in one hand and the broken guitar in the other.

A crop duster flies low across the dark field as pensive Elder Hadley steps up the dusty road. He finds himself face to face with Robert Johnson. Robert hands the clergyman his hoe.

ROBERT (quietly)

I ain't afraid like that.

Robert stares at the preacher, drops his eyes, exits. The gentle preacher slowly pivots, leaning on the hoe. He gazes upon Robert, who heads for the twilit shacks among the trees.

We are listening to the preacher's inner monologue.

ELDER HADLEY (off)

You see, I'm a preacher, Elder Hadley, Elder J. J. Hadley. And you know, the Lord called on me once, when I was out there workin' just like you—

16. EXTERIOR. DIRT PATH. TWILIGHT. SILENCE.

Robert walks wearily with his guitar through the purplish, darkening way. Other tired field hands are seen returning to their shacks, as smoke wafts about from small wood fires.

ELDER HADLEY (off)

He called on me once and He told me—in imagination, you know—that He was wantin' me to preach. I told Him I didn't know enough, that I was ignorant and that folks would laugh at me. But He drew up on me so, I prayed—

Silently, a sharecropper riding an old mule laden with long sacks of cotton. Another silent image, of a man singing while playing a "one-string" nailed to a porch post, with his little daughter dressed in red and dancing gaily.

ELDER HADLEY (off)

I prayed out in them Piney Woods, I prayed
and prayed—

Robert comes upon a hogpen. Inside the pen, VIRGINIA
TRAVIS holds an oval basin filled with water. She is a
slender beauty, no older than seventeen. Robert eyes her
as she quietly sprinkles the dusty pen with water.

ELDER HADLEY (off)

And at last a great light came down to me, and
struck me hard on the head and the shoulder
and the breast, here and here and here, in
imagination, like I said—

She looks up. Their eyes meet.

ELDER HADLEY (off)

And then the same time warmth was in around
my heart. And I felt the Book was there, in my
heart. And I knowed, when I come through it
an' was endowed with the Holy Ghost, I didn't
know nothin'.

Hesitantly, Virginia shifts her attention to her chore.
She does not seem to notice Robert walking away.

ELDER HADLEY (off)

But my tongue was untied, and I'm preachin'
ever since and I ain't afraid. No, Robert, I ain't
afraid.

She turns her head to look after Robert as he walks into
the shadows. A dreamlost old man strolls by with his
fishing pole and string of fish.

17. EXTERIOR. SHACK. NIGHTFALL.

A faceless shack, dark inside and apparently moribund, with wooden steps missing on the front porch. The old fellow with the string of fish pokes by.

We hear strange twanging sounds from within.

18. INTERIOR. SHACK. NIGHTFALL.

The moonlit floor slants toward the opposite corner of the room, where Robert sits facing the converging walls. He is shirtless; his white shirt hangs nearby from a hook.

Robert wraps the guitar box with cord to tighten the fractured wood. He tests the instrument by plucking the strings, then by putting the guitar to his ear.

He warms up with an easy rolling riff, tapping his foot gently, leaning forward. Baring a silvery blade, he runs it down the guitar neck and suddenly back again. The sound is like a smothered shriek.

Virginia appears outside the open window. Hearing the sounds, she pauses, the water basin on her hip.

Robert waxes his guitar strings with a candle that he puts back on a table behind him.

Virginia stands in the doorway.

ROBERT

How old are you?

VIRGINIA

Fifteen.

ROBERT

Better you come in then. Tell me who you are.

VIRGINIA

Virginia, Travis. From Commerce. Abbay-Leatherman plantation.

Robert, always facing the wall, shifts in his chair to the left and starts picking the strings delicately.

Virginia crosses the floor and puts the water basin down behind Robert. She circles behind him quietly. Standing at the table, she lights his candle.

ROBERT

Boyfriend back home?

VIRGINIA

No. I don't belong to anyone personal.

ROBERT

Ain't jealous if you did.

Robert turns around to steal a glimpse of Virginia, who shifts her gaze out the window.

He nudges his chair toward the middle of the room, next to the water basin, then stares obliviously again at the wall.

ROBERT

I'm Robert . . . Johnson. Robert Lonnie Johnson. One of the famous Johnson boys. Robert's me an' Lonnie's from my brother.

VIRGINIA

Lonnie Johnson your kin?

ROBERT

Brother. Distant brother.

VIRGINIA

Tommy Johnson too?

ROBERT

Cousin, mostly. But I learnt the main tricks on Son House.

VIRGINIA

Where's your mother at?

ROBERT

Charley Patton taught me how to spread my hands.

VIRGINIA

Said, where's your mama?

ROBERT

I'm as good as they come. And you a womanly stranger.

VIRGINIA

You avoidin' me.

ROBERT

Ain't avoidin' you at all.

VIRGINIA

Where's your papa?

ROBERT

Why you askin' questions, girl? They dead, all
of 'em. This room here full of 'em. Only I'm
gonna get out, same way I come. This time
where I'm goin' I ain't never comin' back.

Virginia, mystified, stands behind Robert.

VIRGINIA

Where's that?

ROBERT

Chicago.

Head down, Robert strums the guitar, humming softly.
Lowering the guitar to the water's surface, he uses the
basin to create a shimmering resonance.

VIRGINIA

You make them records for Mr. Speir?

ROBERT

Some, a couple. Can't talk about 'em now. Any-
ways, I ain't as good as some of the others, ones
like Son here, or Scrappy Blackwell.

VIRGINIA

Then who you as good as?

ROBERT

You.

Robert lays the guitar on top of the basin.

ROBERT

You goin' with me?

He turns to see Virginia drifting toward the door. We hear faint whooping and singing from outside.

VIRGINIA

You ain't so good as Willie Brown, neither.

ROBERT

You goin' with me?

VIRGINIA

I think your mama now suits you better. Next time at the jook maybe you tell me who you are.

Virginia exits.

19. EXTERIOR. FISH FRY. NIGHT.

A throng of hungry sharecroppers huddles eagerly over a skillet sizzling with catfish.

A spring-driven, upright Victrola has some folks dancing to a popular blues. Gangly, cross-eyed T-Bone has everyone laughing with a hilarious shimmy-she-wa-wa.

VICTROLA (off)

"There's no use of lovin', I don't see where I should,/ So what's the use of lovin' when it don't mean you no good—"

Virginia approaches. Then, abruptly, she reverses herself and heads back to the run-down shack.

20. INTERIOR. SHACK. NIGHT.

Virginia speaks as soon as she reaches the door.

VIRGINIA

The water's for—your feet.

The room is empty. The water basin remains in place on the floor. Standing vertically inside it, partially sub-merged in the water, is the broken guitar.

We hear the Victrola amid the gaiety outside.

VICTROLA (off)

"Oh do that thing, Mr. Lonnie Johnson! The man with nine different feelings, and he puts it in the same place every time!"

21. EXTERIOR. LAKE LANDSCAPE. NIGHT.

Around the black crescent lake wanders the solitary Robert Johnson.

22. EXTERIOR. GRAVEYARD. NIGHT.

CLOSEUP of an old wooden grave marker. Each line of the epitaph is carved crudely into the separate slats.

GRAVE MARKER

Sunday
July 10, 1923
Peyton is no more
Aged 42
Though he was a bad man in many respects
an yet he was a most excellent field
hand, always at his
post.
On this place for 24 years.

Except the measles an its sequence, the
injury rec'd by the mule last Nov'r an its sequence,
he has not lost 15 days' work, I verily believe, in
the remaining 19 years. I wish we could hope for
his eternal state.

Footsteps in the grass. Then someone wearing torn trousers and high black field boots steps across the screen, blocking our view of the marker momentarily. His guitar is set against the side of the marker as he commences to work.

Elderly IKE ZINNERMAN takes care of the overgrown graveyard. The tall man first pulls some weeds up from around a particular grave. He sits on a tombstone inscribed "MAMIE ZINNERMAN—Good Wife" and removes his boots.

Slipping a gray sack over his shoulder, Ike walks to an old tree and starts removing clumps of moss from the overhanging limbs.

Ike struggles with some moss stuck on a distant branch. After he finally removes the gray clump, he stops and stares upward.

High overhead, a heavy rope tangled and bunched at its dangling end.

More footsteps. Ike looks to his side and finds Robert staring up at the rope with him.

IKE (softly)

Had a nephew of mine to get lynched. Wasn't
hardly seventeen years. Named Robert Lee. Returned home one Saturday night and some
white boys beat him to death with an iron rod.
Then laid his body 'cross the track for a train to

run over. White boys went home and went to
bed and that was it. My nephew'd reckoned
those fellas were his friends. They was raised
up together. You find some things in this life on
earth can make you mean.

Ike resumes his moss gathering. He pulls down another
heap with a stick and stuffs it into his sack.

IKE

So if it ain't Mr. Downchild.

ROBERT

What's happenin', Ike?

IKE

Same ol' shit. Workin' from can to cain't. Col-
lectin' this moss here so's I can fix me a new
mattress. How 'bout yourself?

ROBERT

Oh, dark to dark, treadin' the mill. Playin' guitar now.

IKE

Heard somethin' 'bout that. You givin' up harp?

Robert reclines in the graveyard's tall grass.

ROBERT

I'm givin' up everything.

IKE

'Cept the womens.

Ike stuffs the last batch of moss into his sack and walks into the graveyard. He grabs his guitar and sits on Mamie Zinnerman's tombstone, near Robert, who is flat on his back. Ike tunes the guitar.

IKE

Yeah. Give some tightenin' 'round the neck an' shoulders some. There. Huh. Says, "I'm good enough if you are."

Picking the guitar gently, Ike sings a solemn lament in his sensitive, gruff baritone, "Shorty George."

IKE (sadly)

"Lord, what's the matter now?/ Can't read no letter, Lord,/ Don't need no letter nohow—"
(spoken)
Found ol' Nat Walker Sunday mornin', Robert. Wasn't quite dead. Rushed him over to the doctor, but—it's dangerous livin' by yourself alone.

Ike hands his guitar to Robert down in the grass. He picks some more weeds off the grave as Robert picks on the guitar.

IKE

Now Mamie here was different. Even when she got to be so super-annuated an' all, nothin' changed: she was like about the contrariest woman I ever did know. Thought she didn't even need to die. Well—

ROBERT

Maybe she ain't down there.

IKE

Well, maybe she ain't. But I can hear her still, if
I takes a notion. Mmmm. A person don't always
die too fast, if you know what I mean.

Ike scoops up some dirt and puts it in his pocket. He sits
on the tombstone as Robert picks on the guitar.

IKE

One last thing, 'fore ol' Icarus call it a night.
Won't be long 'fore you play gui-tar good like
you do harp. Then you starts gettin' all hot to
go, ramblified y'know like I once was. That time
come, don't you lay your gui-tar down for no
one, Robert—no man or no woman. You can bet
those friendly strangers be comin' your way
with their helpin' hands, someone sayin' they
really found you. Now that jus' hoodoo, boy—
bunch o' lies. Ain't he or she or them or it that
you belong to. Only lead you straight to hell.

Robert sits up and watches Ike put on his boots. We see
the soles have two heels each, facing in opposite directions.

IKE

Got to take care—these Piney Woods eat meat.

Ike slowly trudges toward the graveyard gate.

IKE

Night, son.

ROBERT

Night.

23. INTERIOR. IKE'S SHACK. NIGHT.

From within the eerie darkness we see Ike arrive. He enters the bedroom, leans his guitar against the wall, sits on his bed to remove his boots, and prays.

In a corner, a gray rat snoozes in one of Ike's hats.

IKE (hushed)

"The Lord is my shepherd, I shall not want. He make me to lie down in green pastures, He lead me by the still water, He restore my soul—"

Ike stuffs his mattress with moss. Then he strips naked, sneaks a hit of booze and gets into bed.

IKE (hushed)

"Though I walk through the shadow of Death, I will fear no Evil, for Thou is with me. Thy rod and Thy staff they comfort me. Amen."

Ike falls asleep. Seconds pass. Then, inexplicably, the sound of a random picking at the strings of his guitar. Ike sits up. The picking has gone away.

Fearfully, he prays.

IKE (hushed)

"Thou anointeth my head with oil, my cup runneth over. Goodness and mercy shall follow me all the days of my life, and I shall dwell in the house of the Lord forever."

Ike reclines. The guitar starts to play again. Ike sits up. The playing stops. Ike looks around, then lies back down.

IKE (hushed)

That you, Mamie? Huh? You forget what things
is like down here? Hush up so's I can get my
rest. I ain't been playing none of them blues,
don't you worry—

The guitar falls over with a crash.

Ike struggles out of bed. The guitar is inert. Ike picks it
up and leans it against the wall. Then he returns to bed.

A scratch and a twang. Ike jumps up.

IKE (hushed)

Now I's gettin' right smart. You listen to me. I
been good, leadin' a clean an' humble life, an' I
don't need you remindin' me how fearful and
lonesome things here really is. So lay off,
woman, 'fore I—damn.

More shrill now, the strings are being picked higher up
on the guitar neck. Ike grabs the guitar by the neck and
squeezes hard.

IKE (hushed)

You hear me, Mamie? I warned you. I warned
you, girl. Just remember you still my wife—you
hear me now? Huh? Mamie?
                (pause)
Is that you, Mamie? Or's that, someone else,
maybe—
                (pause)
Lord Jesus. Oh no—gotta do somethin'. Oh
Lord—

Ike stands and reaches for his clothes. He dresses as he
takes the guitar and moves toward the door.

IKE (hushed)

I swear. I swear, Mamie. I swear, darlin'—

He leaves the shack for the fields, guitar in hand.

24. EXTERIOR. GRAVEYARD. MIDNIGHT.

Robert, asleep on his back, hears Ike's footsteps and stands. A worried Ike trudges straight to Mamie's grave, where he sets the guitar against her tombstone. He turns and trudges off again, staring at Robert with eyes of Fear.

ROBERT

So long, Ike.

IKE

You still callin' me that.

ROBERT

Icarus.

IKE

Like in the Bible.

Ike exits. Robert sits, his back against Mamie's tombstone, holding the guitar. He starts picking gently on it, then gradually gains strong momentum by strumming.

25. EXTERIOR. GRAVEYARD. MORNING.

Sitting against the tombstone as before, Robert is strumming furiously, still gaining momentum.

As Robert begins to hoot and holler, a panel truck slows to a halt on the nearby gravel road.

TRUCK DRIVER (off)

Sixty-one! Dockery, Klein plantations! Clarksdale-Greenwood!

FIELD HAND (off)

Hey! Charley Patton!

Laughter. Robert walks toward the truck.

26. EXTERIOR. COTTON GIN. NOON.

The gin activity is noisy and frenzied. Powerful suction pipes scour wagons piled high with cotton. Loud air blasts, and huge snowy white drifts overhead.

Robert hops off the truck, which is loaded immediately with cotton by muscular workers, constantly shouting. Robert looks around, strums the guitar, starts to wander out the main gate. A WORKER shouts at him.

WORKER

Mornin', Miss Lookingood! Kiss my ass, I wish you would!

27. EXTERIOR. GREENWOOD. AFTERNOON.

Robert strolls along the main street in the black quarter. A few blocks ahead, a boisterous mob is kicking up some dust. Robert strums his guitar while walking, as before.

Stopping in front of a bar, he sings a pleasant verse from a familiar blues to himself.

ROBERT (singing)

"Got them blues, can't be satisfied./ Keep them blues, I'll catch that train an' ride—"

Robert stops singing, picking the guitar fluidly as passers-by head up the street toward the mob. We hear the gruff voice of a preacher bellow forth.

CHARLEY PATTON (off)

O Lord, give Thy servant the wisdom of the owl! Connect his spirit to the gospel telephone in the central skies! Lighten his brow with the sun of heaven, poison his mind with love for the people! Turpentine his imagination an' grease his lips with possum oil!

28. INTERIOR. BAR. AFTERNOON.

Leaning on the bar, Robert jaws with the BARTENDER.

ROBERT

You put up some of that Koo Koo hootch, I be fillin' up this place in no time. I be playin' out front an' then you see.

BARTENDER

That's Charley Patton out there too, you know. Bertha Lee, Henry Sims playin' side.

Robert's brow furrows but he tries to appear unimpressed.

ROBERT

You listen here, fish lips—I'm here to headhunt that sonofabitch.

In a dark corner of the bar, a thin, mangy guy wearing a dark hat and sunglasses sits with a bottle of whiskey. He is laughing to himself rather manically, savoring some sort of secret, evil glee, swigging drink after drink.

BARTENDER (off)

Oh yeah?

ROBERT (off)

You see.

BARTENDER

That's Charley *Patton* outside—

The bartender pours Robert a drink as the mangy guy finishes his bottle.

29.   EXTERIOR. GREENWOOD. AFTERNOON.

CHARLEY PATTON sings and dances wildly for the mob with buxom BERTHA LEE and sullen HENRY SIMS. The small Patton is a bizarre ancestral hybrid with copper-colored skin, thick lips and wavy blond hair, wearing a tight urchin's suit and crooked bow tie.

His relentless movements are strange and unpredictable, albeit inevitably lewd. Singing like a wounded bear, he heaves his guitar overhead, catches it behind his back, then runs it suggestively between his legs.

Bertha Lee wears a cowbell around her neck, dances about and tries to keep time on tambourine. Sims plays a strident violin made from a cigar box.

Charley prances and runs rampant, beating up frequently on his partners. The drunken, antic crowd loves it.

CHARLEY (singing)

"I'm runnin' wild, oh I agree,/ That mighty boy, mighty boy, he's runnin' wild—"

The mob swells steadily with men, women, children, white people as well as black, dogs, mules, and so on.

Charley confronts a woman with his pelvis, performing a mock-sexual act as Henry dips in between them and Bertha Lee starts ringing her bell.

> CHARLEY (singing)
>
> "In all my dreams, in all my dreams/ That mighty boy, that mighty girl, he's runnin' wild—"

He leads into a new song by shifting rhythms on guitar, never missing a beat. Playing the long introduction to "Shake It and Break It," he leads the mob up the street.

30. INTERIOR. BAR. AFTERNOON.

Robert downs another drink, still bulling with the bartender. We hear a distant, rhythmic strumming on guitar, and the oncoming mob.

> ROBERT
>
> I's young, but I seen everythin'. Just seen a woman shot at a jook up the country, .44 bullet shot all through. I was playin' an' jumped out the back door. Got in my car and pulled out. Moved so fast I run over don't-know-how-many folks in that ol' racer. I had a racer then.

The bartender pours another drink as the mob outside approaches. Robert, worried, gulps it down.

> ROBERT
>
> 'Bout time I go get 'im—

Just as Robert grabs his guitar and makes for the door,

Charley Patton bursts in with his rough and raucous mob, stampeding the bar and pinning Robert to a chair.

CHARLEY (singing)

"You-can-shake-it-you-can-break-it-you-can-hang-it-on-the-wall/ But I don't wanna catch it 'fore it fall./ My jelly, my roll, sweet mama, don't you let it fall—"

The bar is rocking as Charley leaps atop the bar and, drinking whiskey like water, struts and shouts and carouses while performing the song.

Bertha Lee sits cursing and drinking with the mangy guy in the corner, while Charley lies on his back feigning masturbation atop the bar.

Drunk and staring determinedly at Charley, Robert gets set to challenge him with his guitar. The bartender sees this and whispers into Charley's ear.

BARTENDER

Young nigger over there 'bout to headhunt you, Charley—

Charley twists and jumps onto Robert's table, pummeling him with song, forcing Robert back into his seat.

CHARLEY (singing)

"You-can-scratch-it-you-can-grab-it-you-can-break-it-you-can-twist-it/ A-ny-ways I loves to git it, I/ Had I my right mind I, be worried sometime—"

He sings down mercilessly at Robert, who cannot move, caught in his own nightmare.

CHARLEY (singing)

"I, ain't got nobody here, but me an' myself I/
Stay blue all the time I, aw when the sun go
down./ My jelly, my roll, sweet mama, don't
you let it—"

The uproarious bar crowd urges Charley on.

31. EXTERIOR. GREENWOOD STREET. AFTERNOON.

Charley continues to reign over the ever growing mob in
front of a drugstore, singing "Bo Weavil Blues."

CHARLEY

"Well, I saw the bo weavil, Lord, a-circle,
Lord, in the air, Lordy./ Next time I seed 'im
he had his family there, Lordy—"

Robert mixes with the riotous throng, excited by the extraordinary rhythm of the song. He is burning with a
thirst for revenge.

As the performance ensues, Robert attempts to hurl the
ritualistic "dozens" at the singer, raging at him.

ROBERT

You so filthy all them ants in your pants standin'
in line! Your drawers got so many holes when
you walks they whistle!

His lame effort is lost in the din to all but Charley. The
retort comes by way of improvised song.

CHARLEY (singing)

"Bo weavil fucked your mama way upon the
telephone line, Lordy./ Charley come make her
pussy climb higher an' higher-high, Lordy—"

Robert looks around helplessly as the show goes on. He starts pushing through the crowd, leaving.

32.   INTERIOR. CONJUROR'S LOBBY. LATE AFTERNOON.

A dingy lobby with folding chairs, a dead potted palm, and a counter with a sign reading "Grinding" overhead.

Robert enters. As a sweet old lady places knife after knife on the counter for sharpening, Robert enters a curtained doorway in the rear.

33.   INTERIOR. CONJUROR'S DEN. LATE AFTERNOON.

The tiny, pale green cubicle is large enough for a small table replete with mason jars, animal skulls, hex objects, and a brass scale. A sign on a wall says: "Navigare necesse est. Vivare no est necesse."

A kindly-looking man looks up as Robert peeks in.

ROBERT

You the conjuror?

CONJUROR

Evenin'. What is it, sonny—love or money?

ROBERT

Both. But I needs help with my guitarmanship first.

CONJUROR

A bit more earnin' power, I see. Alrighty. Come in, put your hands up so's I can weigh 'em.

Robert has his hands weighed on the brass scale.

44

CONJUROR

Mmmm, no problem. You need a good, strong hand, and I's got the one that's 'specially for you.

He displays a shiny dime affixed to a metal chain.

CONJUROR

Goes on the left ankle. Wear it wherever you go, there'll be no lackin' for appreciation. Guaranteed. Now, what about that lil fairo you mentioned?

ROBERT

Brownskin, name's Virginia—

CONJUROR

Old situations gotta have old medicines. Like the song says, "Don't you worry." Put your hands up like so an' she'll be crawlin' back 'fore you say "Lemon Jefferson." Mmm. A "John Concubine"—

After glancing at Robert's upraised palms, the conjuror puts a swatch of threadbare cloth on the table. He dips his fingers into jars labeled "BONE" and "BIRD PARTS," sprinkling the powdered stuff onto the swatch. He folds it, runs a string through the knotted ends, and hands it over to Robert.

CONJUROR

You be givin' it back to her in no time—

34.   EXTERIOR. GREENWOOD STREET. LATE AFTERNOON.

Strumming his guitar with added confidence, Robert marches back toward the Charley Patton mob.

Charley and Bertha Lee are performing "Pony Blues."
The crowd's fever is at its peak, as Charley and Bertha
Lee start shoving each other indignantly.

CHARLEY (singing)

"'Hello, Central, what's the matter with your
line?/ Come a storm last night an' tore the
wire down—'"

Charley yanks Bertha Lee's cowbell off and puts it
around his neck, mimicking her. She yanks it back, then
hauls off and punches Charley hard on the jaw. He goes
down twitching, flat on his back, out cold.

Robert, forcing his way in, surges forward, strumming
his guitar to challenge Charley. But he sees Charley
being dragged off unconscious to the bar instead.

Guitar in hand, Robert stands helplessly as the crowd
disperses. Through the passing figures we notice the
mangy guy from the bar, a big bottle of whiskey at his
side, looking on.

VOICE (off)

Someday I wanna be a great, great man like
Charley is—

Robert turns and walks alone up the darkening street.

35.   EXTERIOR. MOVIE HOUSE. TWILIGHT.

With the guitar slung onto his back, a weary and
drunken Robert staggers over to the Paramount movie
house.

MARQUEE
THE PAINTED DESERT
Wm. Boyd—C. Gable

46

The colorful marquee is suddenly illuminated.

36. INTERIOR. MOVIE HOUSE. FILM IN PROGRESS.

Robert clumsily makes his way to a seat in the second row. The chamber flickers with the black and white film, a corny Western.

The mangy guy from the bar enters and stands beneath a lighted "Exit" sign. He slides along the second row and sits down next to Robert, who stares wide-eyed at the screen.

The stranger stares at the flickering screen, still wearing his hat and shades. He takes an enormous hit off his whiskey bottle, then passes it to Robert.

Mesmerized by the movie, Robert slowly raises the bottle to his lips and takes an interminable draft. He slowly lowers the bottle.

The mangy guy, staring forward, leaning to his left toward the oblivious Robert, speaks.

DEVILMAN

I'm blue—I'm black—and I never did make myself.

MOVIE IMAGE: A blinding sunrise.

Robert hands the bottle back, stealing a glimpse of the stranger.

ROBERT

You a devilman.

DEVILMAN

You jus' call me . . . Dutch Boy.

The devilman touches his shades and grimaces. Robert wipes his mouth with his white kerchief.

DEVILMAN

I go down Charlie's Trace, midnight. You get there ten minutes shy so you know you're there. You go to where a road crosses that way, where a crossroads is, with your guitar you get there. I'll walk up, take your guitar, tune it up, then I do somethin' with it an' hand it back, after I played it. You make any ol' tangled-up song you want, don't care what.

Robert is swooning from drink and sleeplessness. As he nods out, the devilman removes his shades to wipe them on his shirt. As he stares straight ahead, we see blind eyes white with cataracts. He puts the shades back on. Robert opens his eyes, barely.

MOVIE IMAGE: A beautiful saloon madam descends her staircase toward the roomful of cowboys below.

DEVILMAN (off)

Midnight.

DISSOLVE.

37. INTERIOR. OLD WEST OPERA HOUSE. BLACK AND WHITE.

DREAM IMAGE: We are seated in an ornate, Old West opera house filled with rowdy Delta black men and women. Amid a crowd in great confusion onstage, a man dressed in a black hat and suit shouts through a megaphone.

ANNOUNCER

Brothers an' sisters, playin' for us tonight, Blind Lemon Jefferson!

48

The noise heightens as the house lights are dimmed. A
spotlight hits the stage as Blind Lemon Jefferson is led
out. Someone grabs his guitar away, someone else removes his shirt. His fat body sparkles with sweat.

VOICES (off)

Blind Lemon! Blind Lemon moan!

A second shirtless fat man suddenly goes barreling into
Blind Lemon. The house goes wild as the stage clears
for the wrestlers. The second man has fallen on young
Lemon, who flails spastically in crawling away.

The second man is blind as well. Each wrestler is on his
knees, not knowing where the other is. The spotlight
chases them as a shower of coins pelts the stage. The audience is in a howling uproar.

With his opponent lost on his knees to the rear, Blind
Lemon crawls to the edge of the stage and shouts in
his high-pitched voice from the footlights.

BLIND LEMON

Preachers, teachers, you's wrong to turn me
over to justice! I never been a Christian! My
folk sing under torture! I sincerely don't know
none of them laws! I ain't you! I just ain't feelin'
so good, this not bein' my home—

DISSOLVE.

DEVILMAN (off)

You get there.

38. INTERIOR. MOVIE HOUSE. FILM IN PROGRESS.

MOVIE IMAGE: Beyond the broad, dusty plains, the towering mountains explode sky-high from dynamite. The movie is over.

The color image returns as Robert wakes with a start. He looks to the empty seat beside him and remembers the devilman. He also remembers the dream.

39.   EXTERIOR. MOVIE HOUSE. NIGHT.

Leaving the theater, Robert seems confused to see that night has fallen. He begins walking up the chilly, desolate street, when his eyes are drawn to something across the way.

A hulking black man struggles out of a tenement doorway. We cannot see his face, but the dissolute blind man is cradling a guitar. He feels his way into an alley and disappears.

40.   EXTERIOR. CHARLIE'S TRACE. MIDNIGHT.

A road sign reads: CHARLIE'S TRACE.

The camera slowly dollies down the ghostly, dirt-paved artery. Anonymous black men walk or stand stationary at points along the way.

Now the road becomes barren. At a dark crossroads we behold Robert Johnson, picking on his guitar nervously, delicately. It is out of tune. Then, footsteps, up the road.

The devilman weaves and stumbles into view. He never looks at Robert, only at his guitar. He takes it, tunes it, turns around and plays an extraordinary guitar part. He hands it back and starts to go.

DEVILMAN

I's so broke, can't even buy my dick a doughnut.

Robert fishes in his pocket, then tosses a coin onto the dirt road. The devilman stoops to pick it up. He tips his hat, stumbling off into the night.

> DEVILMAN
>
> Talk some shit, man, talk some shit—

SILENT IMAGE: Robert, on his knees at crossroads, in the midst of a furious riff on his guitar.

DISSOLVE.

41. INTERIOR. JOOK JOINT. NIGHT.

SILENT IMAGE: An anonymous, dimly lit jook joint somewhere in the Delta. A chaos of dancing sharecroppers, not one of whom seems familiar to us.

Two black youths seated on chairs, playing guitars, entertain the crowd. One of them laughs and pinches his nostrils while he sings. The second one skims what seems to be an animal bone across the guitar strings.

Robert, his skin dirty and his clothes unkempt, looking somewhat tired, sits near the musicians. His furtive eyes never stray from the two guitarists' hands.

DISSOLVE.

42. INTERIOR. BARRELHOUSE. NIGHT.

SILENT IMAGE: Robert, more tired and unkempt than before, sits in a crowded roadside shanty guzzling down a bottle of whiskey as he studies a bottleneck guitar-barrelhouse piano duet by two more youths.

A painted wench sits down and puts an arm around Robert, then props her breast on his shoulder. He does not blink an eye. She licks his ear.

DISSOLVE.

43.   EXTERIOR. LEVEE TENT. LATE NIGHT.

SILENT IMAGE: Kerosene lamps hang from a sagging canopy, as brawny black levee workers bump and grind drunkenly with their female visitors from town. The driving beat is provided by a young man pounding a snare drum and an old-timer blowing and hooting on a fife.

Robert sits alone by the Mississippi River, writing something down in a small black book. He puts the book aside and works at his guitar.

Gamblers crouch nearby shooting craps beneath a lantern. The desperate guy with a gun and all the winnings rolls again, sitting on the neck of some unconscious loser.

A soused worker carries his girl to the river and dumps her in. She staggers ashore and embraces him.

Robert looks on. Haggard almost beyond recognition, he slings the guitar onto his back and exits.

DISSOLVE.

44.   EXTERIOR. COTTON FIELDS. DAY.

The field hands labor in the oppressive heat. A truck rumbles in from the distant levee. As it chugs past, we see Robert asleep with his guitar in the rear.

DISSOLVE.

45.   EXTERIOR. LAKE LANDSCAPE. NIGHT.

A nighthawk coos and flaps its wings against the air, as Robert wanders homeward around the black crescent lake seen earlier.

52

46. INTERIOR. JOOK JOINT. NIGHT.

Son House and Willie Brown are playing and shouting
their blues amid a dancing mob dizzy with momentum.

WILLIE (singing)

"Can't tell my future, I can't tell my past./
Lord, it seem like every minute sure gonna be
my last—"

SON (singing)

"Oh, the blues is a worried heart, a worried
heart disease,/ Like the woman you lovin' so
doggone hard to please—"

Son slides his glass bottleneck over the guitar strings.
He tightens the cloth wrapping that he uses now to pro-
tect his hand from the jagged glass.

47. EXTERIOR. WOODED CLEARING. NIGHT.

Robert kneels not far from the jook with his guitar,
which he is ready to play with a knife-slide. His black
book lies open by his knee next to a whiskey bottle.

Robert looks around, then reaches for a dried rabbit's
carcass. He takes a quick hit of whiskey and rips the
dead creature apart with the knife. He chooses a good
bone and cuts the flesh away. Then he hollows out the
marrow, making it smooth, and slips the new slide onto
his finger.

We observe Robert kneeling in the clearing from afar.
He runs the shiny wet bone slide up the neck of his guitar, then listens to the startling, weird sounds fade to
nothing. He lights a match and starts to dry the bone
slide.

48. INTERIOR. JOOK JOINT. NIGHT.

With both musicians continuing to play guitar to keep the furious dance rhythm intact, Son shouts out an introduction for a new number.

SON (shouting)

This one's on me, just as well as admit it! This is the truth! Course, some of it's a little addition, but the biggest of it's the truth, 'cause I'm a preacher! Least I was 'fore I started this junk!

WILLIE (shouting)

Lord have mercy!

SON (singing)

"Gonna get me religion, gonna join the Baptist Church,/ Gonna be a Baptist preacher so's I sure won't have to work—"

The guitar slung onto his back, Robert stands in the doorway eyeing the musicians. Son continues to sing as Willie spots Robert and eyes him back.

SON (singing) (off)

"Well, I met the blues this mornin', walkin' just like a man—"

WILLIE (off)

Son!

SON (singing) (off)

"Said, 'Good mornin', blues, give me your right hand—'"

54

WILLIE (off)

Son! Look who's comin' in the door—

Robert works his way through the crowd, past a wench atop a table stooping down upon a dime.

SON (off)

Yeah, it's Little Robert—

WILLIE

An' he's got hisself a gui-tar!

The musicians are roaring with laughter while trying to maintain the intensity of the performance. Robert, his appearance messy, confronts the laughing men with a deadly look in his eye.

SON (laughing)

Well, boy, you got a gui-tar, huh—what you do with that thing?

WILLIE (laughing)

You can't do nothin' with it!

·The guitar playing continues as Robert stares at Son.

ROBERT

Well, I'll tell you what.

SON

Now what's that?

ROBERT

Let me take your seat a minute.

WILLIE

Hooo-boy!

ROBERT

Said I'm takin' your seat, Son.

SON (bemused)

All right, an' you better do somethin' with it,
too—

In the midst of the whirling frenzy, Son stands and
winks at Willie, who looks betrayed. Robert sits down as
Son leaves and Willie soon follows.

49. EXTERIOR. JOOK JOINT. NIGHT.

Son and Willie, overcome with laughter, grab a bottle of
hootch each and drink up.

SON

You seen that boy's face?

WILLIE

'Bout turned black as a ghost when you give it
to 'im!

Stunning guitar sounds cut through the night from the
jook. Robert is playing "Preachin' Blues," astonishing all
with his rhythmic and emotional intensity.

Son and Willie swallow some whiskey and freeze.

SON

Say, what's that—

56

ROBERT (singing) (off)

"Mmmmmmmmm mmmmmmm! I's up this
mornin', the blues, walkin' like a man./ Worried
blues, give me your right hand—"

WILLIE

Holy shit—

50. INTERIOR. JOOK JOINT. NIGHT.

The jammed jook dances madly to the ringing voice and
guitar, a vision of rhythm.

ROBERT (singing)

"The blues grabbed Mama's child, tore it all
upside down./ Travel on, poor Bob, just can't
turn you 'round—"

Glimpses of a possessed Robert through the moving
figures. He is hunched over the guitar, his head thrown
back to sing, his body shifting in the chair with the
rhythm.

ROBERT (singing)

"The blues is a low-down, achin' heart disease/
Like consumption, killing me by degrees—"

51. EXTERIOR. JOOK JOINT. NIGHT.

Son and Willie follow Robert out of the jook.

SON

Now ain't that somethin' fast—

Each grabs a bottle of hootch at the stand.

WILLIE

What you talkin' 'bout that trick, anyway?

SON

How'd you do it, Robert?

ROBERT (to Son)

Just like you.

WILLIE (muttering)

Man, it wasn't yet a year ago—

Robert starts drifting away. Son catches up and walks through the crowd alongside him.

SON

Now, Robert, you go 'round playin' these Saturday night balls, let me give you some instruction—

Robert ignores him, lost in another world, drinking.

SON

See, you got to be careful 'cause you mighty crazy 'bout the girls. When you playin' an' they's full of that corn whiskey an' snuff all mixed together, an' you be playin' a good piece they like an' come up an' call you, "Daddy, play it again, Daddy"—well, don't let it run you crazy, or—

Seeing beautiful Virginia Travis standing off to the side with another man, Robert leaves Son.

SON (off)

—you liable to get killed.

Robert and Virginia face each other. Robert glares at the other man as Virginia takes Robert's hand.

Son looks on as Willie steps up.

WILLIE

Little Robert. Huh.

Robert leads Virginia away from her defeated friend.

SON (off)

He's gone now—

52. EXTERIOR. FIELD NEAR SHACK. LATE NIGHT.

In the distance, Robert and Virginia walk hand in hand toward the glowing shack beyond. Robert stops and embraces Virginia. They kiss.

ROBERT

You goin' with me?

VIRGINIA

Robert, I don't know who you are or nothin' really about you, 'cept I knows I'm supposed to go with you, yes.

They start walking onward toward the shack.

VIRGINIA

When a man goes down his road, he goes with a friend.

53.   INTERIOR. SHACK. LATE NIGHT.

A noisy house party in a nicely furnished shack. More wild dancing, this time to a rocking jug band recording played on an upright Victrola.

In the corner, Robert's stout half sister HERCULES is plucking a makeshift bass when she spots Robert.

> HERCULES
>
> You call it a garbage can, I calls it a streamline bass!

She rushes over to greet Robert, making him dance.

His brother-in-law GRANVILLE follows suit with Virginia. Looking worried, Robert strains to keep an eye on his guitar while he dances.

> HERCULES
>
> My baby half brother Robert Dusty!

> ROBERT
>
> Sweet sister Hercules!

> HERCULES
>
> So good seein' yo' pretty face! Who that angel chile, lookin' so like yo' mama Julia—somethin' special?

> ROBERT
>
> Yeah, name's Virginia, somethin' real special.

> HERCULES
>
> Whoa now, shake that thing! Dirt an' all, you lookin' good!

54.   EXTERIOR. PORCH. LATE NIGHT.

Through the screen door we see Hercules put her arm
around Virginia and lead her out of view. Granville puts
a hand on Robert's shoulder as they exit.

They sit opposite each other in swinging love seats. Robert tunes his guitar as they talk.

GRANVILLE

Say, Robert, that angel chile you with tonight
. . . somethin'—

ROBERT

Yeah, Granville, she special.

GRANVILLE

Virginia, that's it. Lord, Lord. Little girl's a
livin' doll. You gonna be providin' for her soon?
That's what the womens gotta have, y'know—

ROBERT

That ain't what they gotta have.

VICTROLA (off)

"Since I come o'er here, sweet baby, 'cause
I'm all alone/ Haven't got nobody jus' to
carry my smokin' on./ Won't you draw my
cigarette—"

GRANVILLE

What I'm meanin' to say is, you been helpin'
out the Big Boss lately?

ROBERT

Naw, I don't do that.

GRANVILLE

What you mean, you "don't do that"? Gotta live somehow, y'gotta eat, and if you be thinkin' of providin' for someone else—

ROBERT

I ain't providin' for no bossman no more neither.

GRANVILLE

Like the Good Book say—

ROBERT

—God makes man, man makes money.

GRANVILLE

You reaps what you done sowed.

ROBERT

An' you don't trust a soul.

GRANVILLE

Well, you gotta work for someone.

VICTROLA (off)

"Jus' draw my cigarette, baby, till you make my good ashes come—"

ROBERT

Granville, I'm makin' my resolution. I'll work for that.

GRANVILLE

That's it, Robert. I want you to tell me on your own now.

ROBERT

Well, you may not want to hear it.

GRANVILLE (pen in hand)

I'm writin' it down, you tell it.

ROBERT

I'm goin' to put out a prayer, in the mornin'. I'm gonna tell the Lord to search my heart, an' if He finds anything been hangin' there like a double shovel, a gang plow, a cotton sack, a mule, I want Him to move it, an' cast it into the sea of forgiveness, so it won't rise against me in this world either the world to come.

GRANVILLE (writing)

Huh, now wait a minute—

ROBERT (slowly)

Your soul, it reaps less from knowin' a little gain than losin' a whole lot more, I reckon.

GRANVILLE

You mean that?

ROBERT

I sure do.

GRANVILLE

Then boy, you goin' to hell.

ROBERT

Hell ain't where you dead, Granville. It's where you alive.

Goat, pulling a wooden wagon with a guitar inside, steps off the dark road and goes to the side of the shack.

55. INTERIOR. KITCHEN. LATE NIGHT.

Goat enters the congested kitchen and puts a can on the counter labeled "STERNO/Cooking Fuel." He takes out a rag and some matches, then loosens the lid on the can with his front teeth.

> VICTROLA (off)
>
> "Get off with me! Honey, bend your knee./
> Don't get too drunk 'cause you can't last long./
> Get off with me—"

Robert enters. Goat, still wearing his hare's foot, makes eye contact with him, then narrates the preparation of his poisonous drink. He lights a match.

> GOAT
>
> Y'burn off the top . . . get a good rag, an' strain it . . . it's got juice in it, squeeze it out—

Goat pours the red fuel into the rag, then wrings the liquid into another can. He grabs a sugar jar and two tin cups. Robert pushes through toward Goat.

> GOAT
>
> Sugar . . . water, the way you like it . . . there.

He fills one cup, tastes it approvingly, then fills the second and hands it to Robert. Together they exit via the kitchen door.

56. EXTERIOR. SHACK. LATE NIGHT.

Goat imparts some wisdom to Robert as they wander in darkness toward the road.

GOAT (drinking)

This canned heat'll get that guitar singin' like it should, 'cause mmm! you gotta be open up 'fore you can do any kind of work. The openin's what makes you one of us—

Robert drinks up and almost chokes as ONE-LEGGED SAM staggers out from the shadows on the road. Goat, alarmed, turns Robert around and casually continues talking as they walk toward the shack.

The old cuss Sam hops after them.

ROBERT

Watchit, it's One-Legged Sam—

GOAT

See, whenever you run up on somethin' playin', y'know your changes like it's connectin' somethin' together, y'know how to hold it—

SAM (off)

There you is, Goat! You ain't playin', I's gonna beat yo' ass! I's gonna beat yo' black ass, boy!

GOAT

—but you got to feel it an' get it, it'll mumble through you gradually, then you knows how to run it right. Boogies, blues, it come right to you. That's when you make some money, at that time—

Robert rushes inside. Sam catches up and starts beating up on Goat, too drunk to offer resistance, pushing him on toward the shack.

SAM

Go on! Git in, play! Git! Go on—

57. EXTERIOR. PORCH. LATE NIGHT.

Through the screen door we see Sam push Goat into the
main room amid the guests, shoving Goat's guitar into
his gut. Goat can hardly stand up.

SAM (leaving)

You play now 'fore I wipe my nose all over you,
you drunken nigger—

Sam steps outside and stands facing the darkness, arms
crossed. Upon hearing Goat's mellow voice singing and
yodeling "Canned Heat Blues," he nods his head,
satisfied.

GOAT (singing) (off)

"Cryin' canned heat, canned heat, mama, sure
Lord killin' me./ Takes Alcorub to take these
canned heat blues—"

The slightest smile on his face now, Sam does a little
dance on the porch. There is some stifled laughter from
the party inside. Sam stops dancing, suspicious.

We peek through the door with Sam. As the Victrola
plays "Canned Heat Blues," Goat pretends to play the
guitar, mouthing the words. Then he kicks off his
soleless shoes and dances on the guitar, picking the
strings with his toes.

VICTROLA

"Cryin', mama mama mama, cryin' canned heat
killin' me./ Believe to my soul, Lord, it gonna
kill me dead—"

An enraged Sam bursts in as Goat's foot crushes the guitar. Sam drags him roughly outside, throwing him off the porch and tumbling in the dust.

Like a carnivorous beast the amputee beats, bites and kicks Goat, who is too drunk to fathom what is happening. Occasionally he yelps.

The party-goers rush outside. Robert flies off the porch onto Sam's back. Sam brushes him off like a fly while he tries to twist Goat's head off. Goat strains to bite off Sam's fingers. Robert tries to bite off his wooden leg, then grabs it with both hands and rips it off.

As Robert flails clumsily at Sam with his wooden leg Goat bites Sam's nose off. Hercules snatches the leg from Robert and clubs Sam mercilessly.

Sam lies twitching and bleeding on the ground. Hercules returns the wooden leg to Robert, who glares at Sam, and then heaves his leg into the dark field.

58.   INTERIOR. SHACK. WEE HOURS.

Everyone is sprawled about the dim, candlelit room, too tired and drunk to stand. The inebriating early Louis Armstrong recording "Knockin' a Jug" lulls the room to sleep. A drowsy couple has a drunken exchange.

HUSBAND

I'm proud of you, darlin'.

WIFE

I'm tired of you, too, babe.

Robert stares at the far corner with his guitar, his back to the room. The record ends and the needle skips. Robert oversteps bodies and turns the Victrola off.

Granville moans, stirring. Robert talks softly, lulling him back to sleep as he moves slowly toward Virginia.

ROBERT (hushed)

"And the Lord make the earth empty, an' make it waste, an' turn it upside down, an' scatter its childrens all 'round the town, fuck an' kill each other—"

GRANVILLE (mumbling)

"—for the Lord has spoke the word. The earth mourns an', fades, away; the earth, fades—"

Robert kneels beside Virginia, asleep next to Hercules. Her face is wet with tears. She opens her eyes, he takes her by the hand. They exit. The others remain, sleeping on the floor, fetal, like infants.

59. EXTERIOR. LEVEE SLOPE. WEE HOURS.

In soft moonlight, Virginia lies naked on the moist, sloping turf. Robert removes his pants and kneels naked beside her.

Virginia rolls gracefully on top of Robert, kissing his slender body, as he kisses hers.

60. EXTERIOR. LEVEE. BEFORE DAWN.

The levee swells up from the backwater flatlands like an awesome monolith. Leaning against the purple predawn sky, the flood wall seems to prevent the very sun from rising. Crickets punctuate the dark stillness.

The silhouetted figures of Robert and Virginia trek steadily in the distance atop the levee. The camera tracks left to right with them.

VIRGINIA

You been to Alabama, Robert?

ROBERT

Bad place for musicianers. Can't be hangin'
'round no dead folk.

VIRGINIA

You been there?

ROBERT

No.

VIRGINIA

Well, it's beautiful, nothin' like Mississippi at
all. There's a fine big stretch where I was born
at Red Bay; people say they hear things there,
sometimes see a great light. That's what they
say. I seen a whole lotta bones that's been
turned up in the fields. There was an open passage I remember once, goin' down under the
field, an' me an' two girls went in. Saw the
ashes from the fires that the slaves used to
make. The passage is closed now.

Silence. The silhouetted figures continue on.

ROBERT

I seen Chicago myself. Caught sight of it one
time. Had a high steel wall all 'round it, with a
straight walk on top of it, an' inside the wall I—

VIRGINIA

I was dreamin', Robert. Dreamin' I was
dreamin' I was with a tiny child, not a boy an'

not a girl, we was sleepin' somewhere. 'Twas
dark but we knew where we was—

Robert and Virginia pause atop the levee. As they gaze
off in different directions, a sense of emptiness.

The camera joins them on the elevated gravel road, pan-
ning 360° around the dim Delta landscape. We see the
Mississippi River, the black cypress swamps, the levee
road stretching out ahead, the slumbering fields, the
shacks.

Robert bends low and picks up a stone. He tosses it out
over the sullen swamp; we hear a distant splash. Taking
Virginia's hand, he leads her homeward.

          ROBERT (fading)

We goin' to Chicago. They got all kinds of instruments or parts you want up there from
slides to strings, all made of steel. Blind Blake,
Scrappy Black an' a whole lot of 'em, Lou
Armstrong is there. They bug the music, make
you play, see who could cut one another. That's
why you get good, y'know—

They fade into the dimness. We remain, staring at the
swamp, as somewhere a rooster crows. A little sign in
the foreground reads: "Night Travel on Levee Pro-
hibited."

FADE OUT.

61. INTERIOR. SHACK. DAY.

FADE IN.

Robert leaves an inner bedroom as the radio announces
a July 4th sale in Clarksdale. Suspended on the far wall,
a plain white bridal dress and veil.

The camera dollies into the main room, where Robert sits by the Victrola with his guitar, concentrating hard as Skip James's spellbinding "Devil Got My Woman" plays. Hercules passes through to another room.

VICTROLA

"I'd rather be the Devil, to be that woman's man—"

Robert, brow furrowed, hums along with the falsetto voice quietly. Virginia rests behind him on the sofa, uncomfortably, a wet washcloth cooling her brow.

A strange rumbling and sputtering sound emerges from outside. Through the window we see Goat drive up to the shack in a jalopy, with rags on the wheels instead of tires. It is a gray, gloomy day.

Robert concentrates hard by the Victrola as Goat comes inside, carrying a small book. He approaches Robert.

GOAT

Need a paper bag.

Robert points toward the kitchen and Goat exits. He reappears with a brown paper bag, puts the book down next to Robert, and goes outside. The book title reads: *Exegesis of Musical Knowledge.*

Goat lifts up the hood of his car. He leans in, reaching down with the paper bag, then straightens up with the bag soaked in oil. He re-enters the shack.

GOAT

Back a minute.

He goes into the kitchen. Seconds later, smoke drifts out. Goat reappears with two jars filled with a black liquid. He and Robert drink up.

ROBERT

Where's the car from?

GOAT

Jackson. Got it with the money they give me for my rights. An' the book there, too.

VICTROLA

"Aw, nothin' but the Devil changed my baby's mind—"

GOAT

Can't reckon much what it's gettin' at, but it's good to have. It's a book. Let you tell them bass strings from the sopranos.

Through the window we see Lavendar towing One-Legged Sam in the wooden wagon. She drinks from an old oil can while limping down the dirt road.

Granville enters with his elderly friend JACK OWENS, as Robert drinks up and Goat dashes drunkenly out the door after Lavendar.

Big Hercules, her hair pinned and wearing shades, sits down with Virginia. She feels Virginia's forehead as Granville and Jack approach Robert.

GRANVILLE

Afternoon! Like that Skip James you playin'. Jack Owens here, he live up the hills, Bentonia—

Robert finishes his drink while Goat falls trying to crank up his motor. Examining Virginia, Hercules seems alarmed. She glares at Robert, then moves toward him.

> JACK OWENS (off)

Yes, uh-huh, I knows Skippy a bit, play often, you know. I learnt that boy a few things, uh-huh—

Hercules grabs Robert by the collar and hauls him off toward the kitchen, interrupting old Jack abruptly.

> JACK OWENS (off)

"Devil Got My Woman." That's Skippy too, uh-huh. Good tune—

62. INTERIOR. KITCHEN. DAY.

Hercules is angry. Throwing her bulk around, she pushes Robert around the tiny kitchen, scolding him.

> HERCULES

Jus' who you think you are, baby brother? Who you think you are, drinkin' that hootch, stayin' out all night in them jooks, comin' back lookin' like a fright all filthy—huh? Why you beatin' up on Jesus so? Tell me!

> ROBERT (muttering)

Reven—

> HERCULES

An' what about Virginia! Po' child alone on that sofa now sufferin'! Huh? She yo' wife or isn't she? You married, boy, or how come?

ROBERT (muttering)

How co—

Hercules slaps the drunken Robert and pins him against the wall.

HERCULES

You sober up! You quit that devil music an' go out in that field pick cotton like a man! Can't you see she gonna need yo' help? Don't you know what's happenin' to that girl? Can't you tell?

ROBERT

What, she bein' sick—

HERCULES

Sick! You think she's like on her back with fever? That woman's carryin' your child, man! Virginia's pregnant, Robert! You gonna be a *father* soon—

Robert, stupefied, is shaken quick.

63. INTERIOR. SHACK. AFTERNOON.

Robert walks to the sofa and sits down on an armrest. He gently pats Virginia's brow.

64. EXTERIOR. PORCH. AFTERNOON.

Jack and Granville sit on the love seats. A little boy watches Granville make him a guitar with fishing line and a cigar box. Jack tunes Robert's guitar.

Granville ties a knot and talks to the boy at his feet.

GRANVILLE

Little boys have to be careful, they can be so triflin' sometimes. In Africa they gets punished when they been bad, folks put 'em on the banjo, that's in yo' grandpappy's time. When he play that night they sing about that boy, tell all about him. That's "puttin' on the banjo," an' that boy sure better change his ways—

Jack shouts out a gripping version of Skip James's song.

JACK (singing)

"Ohhh, it must be the Devil, baby, to be that woman's whoooo—"

DISSOLVE.

65.   EXTERIOR. FOREST. NIGHT.

In a clearing, the tall dark evergreens contrast with the parched yellow trees. Robert, his guitar leaning against a tree and his black book upside down, paces pensively.

JACK (singing) (off)

"Ohhhh, it must be the Devil, baby, done changed that woman's myyyy—"

DISSOLVE.

66.   EXTERIOR. COTTON FIELD. NOON.

Robert chops and chops with a hoe in the hot fields. Beside him, Granville lustily stuffs his long sack with cotton. Robert's expression is serious, steadfast.

Elder Hadley strolls by in a red sports coat, tipping his hat to the laborers, smiling at Robert. Granville smiles back; Robert looks down and chops harder.

JACK (singing) (off)

"Oh, the Devil got religion, baby, but he joined
no Baptist Church./ The Devil got religion,
baby, but he joined no Baptist ahhhhh—"

DISSOLVE.

67. INTERIOR. BEDROOM. MIDNIGHT.

Robert is asleep with his very pregnant wife. Their
white sheet glows in the moonlight.

Robert opens one eye. He rises, sits on the edge of the
bed with his guitar, stares out the window.

Through the window, an old tree trembles in the
gusty night.

FADE OUT.

68. EXTERIOR. OLD TREE. MORNING.

FADE IN.

Hercules, Granville, Robert and Virginia, all dressed in
their Sunday best, walk under the tree and climb inside
Granville's Model T. The car drives away.

69. EXTERIOR. CHURCH. MORNING.

A small white clapboard church on a hill, shaded by a
chinaberry tree. We hear the congregants singing before
the service is to begin. Granville's car approaches the
church, stopping on the side.

SINGING (off)

"Oh, Lordy, just give me a long white robe, in
the heaven./ Choose your seat an' set down—"

Hercules and Granville greet DEACON L. J. BATES at the door as Robert helps Virginia out of the car. Robert is groomed impeccably in hat, suit with suspenders, white shirt and tie. They approach the deacon.

DEACON

God willing, it won't be long now—You as big as can be, chile!

VIRGINIA

You know, Deacon Bates, I'm thinkin' that there's miracles happenin' in secret all around—

DEACON

That's 'cause you're looking for Deliverance, Mrs. Johnson! But to win Deliverance, you got to wait on the movements of Providence— Robert, mornin', so good to have you with us again!

Robert and Virginia enter the church.

70. INTERIOR. CHURCH. MORNING.

The pews are filled with congregants in song. Hercules leads Granville to a seat up front.

SINGING

"Oh, Jesus, was my mother there?/ In the heaven, choose yo' seat an' set down, trouble over—"

The beautiful singing dissipates while Robert and Virginia slip into seats behind Granville and Hercules.

The entire pulpit is covered with white sheets. The powerful voice of REV. GATES bellows above a few fading singers. From the beginning, his delivery is joined by an increasing number of shouts and cries from inspired congregants (noted in parentheses).

REV. GATES

Now, chillun, I gonna speak the truth! I'm goin' if it takes my life.

CONGREGATION

AMEN!

REV. GATES

I'm goin' every step of the way!
    (Yessuh! Amen!)
I mean sho' 'NUF!
    (Yessuh! TELL IT!)
With FEAR an' with TREMBLING!
    (Yessuh! Amen!)
That I gonna work out my SOUL SALVATION!

CONGREGATION

AMEN (TRUTH!)

REV. GATES

I'm goin' if it TAKES MY LIFE! I don't care what the world may say—I'M GOIN'!

CONGREGATION

YESSUH!

REV. GATES

We have a whole-lotta-peoples-around-here, OHHHH, haven't connected themselves to NOOO church!

(YESSUH! TRUTH!)
An' we have workin' mens an' womens 'round
here, for ten, eleven years an' I KNOW! THEY
HAVEN'T YET ACCEPTED JESUS CHRIST! AN' THE
HAND OF SALVATION! An' there are people 'round
here sayin' they been BORNED again, BUT THERE
BE NO CHURCH A-ROUND 'EM!
(TELL IT!)

CALLETTA CRAFT, a stunning woman of thirty-five who
sits with her two young sons, swoons over a spiritual
threshold into a lilting, cooing musical response.

REV. GATES

But I'm in DOUBT 'bout yo' REGENERATION!
(TELL IT!)

The lilting voice gets stronger, and now a deeper, male
voice joins in. The voices slowly swell toward song behind the shouting and sermonizing.

REV. GATES

YOU HAVEN'T SHOWED AS MUCHA SENSE AS THOSE
LITTLE OL' MICE! I remember one mornin', I
walked into my kitchen, an' the creature had a
CRUMB in his mouth—

Virginia hums fervently as Robert skims the hymnal.
The congregation is beginning to reel hypnotically, led
by Calletta and, now we see, Granville.

REV. GATES

So I RUSHED THE LITTLE OL' MOUSE!

SINGING

Ohhhhhhhhhhh yeahhhhhhhhhhh—

REV. GATES

An' he tried to get through of that hole an' carry the little crumb WITH 'IM! An' I kep' a-rushin' an' he throwed the crumb away an' SAVED HIS LIFE!

SINGING

OHHHHHHHHH, we gonna see, HIMMMMMMM—

REV. GATES

Now there's a whole lotta workin' mens an' womens 'round here tryin' to hold onto their crumbs BUT GOD WILL THROW THEM AWAY! AN' GO TO HEAVEN WITHOUT 'EM!

CONGREGATION

AMEN!

REV. GATES

GOD'LL GO ALONE, HE AIN'T GONNA WAIT! SO THROW 'EM AWAY! YOU GOTTA GO IF IT TAKES YO' LIFE!

Rev. Gates spontaneously bursts into song, waving his arms like an orchestral conductor.

REV. GATES (singing)

"An' I'm goin' if it takes my life"—SING IT!

REV. AND CONGREGATION (singing)

"I'M GOIN' IF IT TAKES MY LIFE./ IF I DIE ON THAT SAD OL' FIELD, I'M GOIN' IF IT TAKES MY LIFE— AMEN!"

Hercules and Granville are bellowing. Virginia, tiny beads of sweat along her brow, sings heartfully. Calletta sings toward Granville, then shifts her gaze to Robert behind him. He does not seem to notice.

REV. GATES

SOMEBODY HERE HAVE TROUBLE IN THEM EYES! SOME MOTHER'S FEARS OF TARNATION: OHHHH-OOOO-OHHHHHH! AN' THERE'S SUN IN SOME DISTANT LAND, AN' THAT SUN IS THE SUN THAT'S BACK ON! I CAN HEAR THEM WHEN THEY CRY—

Robert commences to sing. Granville strains with Faith.

REV. AND CONGREGATION (singing)

"I'M GOIN' IF MY CHILDREN DON'T GO./ I'M GOIN' IF MY CHILDREN DON'T GO./ IF I DIE ON THE SAD OL' FIELD, I'M GOIN' IF MY CHILDREN DON'T GO—"

DISSOLVE.

71. INTERIOR. CHURCH. TWILIGHT.

Rev. Gates chants now with an urgent, dark intensity. An almost sinister tone in his voice and rhythm.

Robert and Virginia are mouthing silent chants with other young congregants, kneeling at a front bench. A pressing mob of older congregants surrounds them. In the dimly lit chamber, a mood of delirious foreboding.

REV. GATES (chanting)

OH-WHEN-THEM-ROMAN-SOLDIERS-COME-RIDING-IN-FULL-SPEED-AN'-PLUNGED-HIM-IN-THE-SIDE-WHEN-THAT-BLOOD-AN'-WATER-COME-OUT-OHHHHHHHHHH-OOHHHHHHH-ALMIGHTY-PLACED-IT-IN-THE-PEOPLE'S-MINDS-THAT-THE-WATER'S-FOR-BAPTISM-AN'-THE-

BLOOD-IS-FOR-CLEANSIN', I-DON'T-CARE-HOW-MEAN-
YOU-BEEN, GOD'S-ALMIGHTY-BLOOD-WILL-CLEANSE-
YOU, GREAT-GOD-WILL-COME—

Virginia is sweating profusely. Robert is oblivious. The mob closes in. The women are moaning. A shriek.

Eyes closed, knees bent, body limp, Calletta enters a sensual trance. Shouts ring out about her. Bedlam.

VOICES

She goin' through! God fly! Holy dance!

DEACON

Holy DANCE!

REV. GATES (off)

THEY-SET-TO-LOOK-ABOUT-THE-TEMPLE, JESUS-SAID-
TO-TEAR-IT-DOWN-AN'-IN-THREE-DAYS-I'LL-RIDE-UP-
AGAIN. HE-WAS-TALKIN'-'BOUT-HIS-TEMPLED-BODY-
HANGIN'-THERE—

Her closed eyelids fluttering, Calletta undulates with slow, sensual abandon. Softly, nearly lost in the din, she mutters her signal that she is possessed. She steps toward Robert with eyes closed, moist lips moving.

CALLETTA

Oh movin' . . . oh, oh under me, oh, oh, papa,
I'm goin', oh God—

With other women lapsing into trances all around her, Calletta is kneeling in front of Robert, leaning backward, her arms outstretched, her breasts heaving.

REV. GATES (off)

—THEY-DIDN'T-KNOW-WHAT-HE-WAS-TALKIN'-'BOUT,
I-SEEN-WHILE-HE-WAS-HANGIN', THEM-MOUNTINGS-
BEGIN-TO-TREMBLE-IN-WHICH-JESUS-WAS-HANGIN'-
ON, BLOOD-WAS-DROPPING-DOWN-THE-MOUNTING,
HOLY-BLOOD-WAS-DROP-PING-DOWN—

Virginia, sweating terribly, cringing, continues to chant silently as Robert beholds Calletta.

REV. GATES (off)

—OUR-MAKER-DYING, CREATOR-OF-THE-SUN, (now singing) OOOOO-OOOOOOOOO! HE-MAKE-THE-MOON—

72. EXTERIOR. CHURCH. NIGHTFALL.

The service is over, as some cooing sighs inside persist. The congregants exit into a light rain, past a conjuror at his stand under an awning, his jars and paraphernalia on display, softly calling.

CONJUROR

Good with two magics better than one. . . .
Good with two magics—

Hercules and Granville rush through the rain to the Model T. Robert, his arm around Virginia, follows. Granville motions for them to hurry.

They get into the car; it sputters away, headlights bouncing. It disappears down the hillside, reappearing on the road below, creeping forward at fifteen miles per hour.

73. INTERIOR. MODEL T. NIGHT.

Granville drives without windshield wipers, singing a responsive duet with Hercules in the front seat.

HERCULES (singing)

"Ohhhh, Lordy, jus' give me a long white robe—"

GRANVILLE (singing)

"In the heaven—"

HERCULES (SINGING)

"Choose yo' seat an' set down—"

GRANVILLE (singing)

"Trouble over—"

In the back seat, Virginia reclines with her head on Robert's lap.

VIRGINIA

Robert—

Robert daydreams out the window. Virginia is in obvious pain, sweating and getting faint.

VIRGINIA

Robert—

ROBERT (gently)

What's happenin', Virginia?

GRANVILLE (off)

I'm throwin' them crumbs away!

HERCULES (off)

Tell it!

VIRGINIA (faint)

Robert, get me to the doctor, Robert—

GRANVILLE

Robert!

HERCULES (singing)

"Ohhhh, Jesus! Was my mother there?"

ROBERT (off)

Granville!

GRANVILLE

Robert, I hear them say that the Devil was in
heaven one time when the people was feelin' in
danger, an' they said the Devil took his tail an'
drug down three thirds of heaven—

ROBERT

GRANVILLE—

GRANVILLE (off)

—which is why the Lord put him in a sealed-up
place where he can't get—

ROBERT

GRANVILLE, STEP ON IT—

GRANVILLE

What's goin' on back there?

Hercules turns to find Virginia in labor.

HERCULES

VIRGINIA!

ROBERT

GRANVILLE! VIRGINIA'S STARTIN' TO PERCOLATE!

VIRGINIA (faint)

Robert, ohhh . . . Jesus, please—

74. EXTERIOR. GRAVEL ROAD. NIGHT.

The Model T creeps through the rain at twenty miles per hour on the pitted road.

75. INTERIOR. MODEL T. NIGHT.

Virginia, moaning softly, struggles with the pain as Robert pats her face with his white kerchief.

HERCULES (singing)

"Ohhh, Lordy, jus' give me a long white robe./ Ohhh, Lordy, jus' give me a long white robe—"

ROBERT

HEAR ME, GRANVILLE? 'GINIA'S PERCOLATIN'! FAST NOW, GRANVILLE, FAST—

GRANVILLE

I heared ya! I'm goin' as fast as I can—

He steps hard on the gas, the engine starts to sputter. The car shows to a halt.

GRANVILLE

Damn. Stalled out. God damn—

Robert is terrified. Virginia writhes on his lap, as Granville and Hercules get out to push. The car rolls, Granville jumps in to start the engine. Nothing. He gets out to push again.

Looking ahead through the wet windshield, the car is pushed forward ever so slowly into the blackness.

VIRGINIA (off)

Oh, Robert . . . hurry. . . .

Finally, a thundering vehicle approaches from the rear. In seconds only, a shiny car roars by with voices hooting and hollering. It speeds away into the night, the voices crying, "NIGGER!"

Robert cradles Virginia as the Model T crawls onward, and sings to her tenderly.

ROBERT (singing)

"Girl, I love you, tell the world I do-heyyy./
Girl, I love you, tell the world I do—"

A black panel truck overtakes the Model T and pulls over fifty yards ahead. The headlights inch toward it.

ROBERT (singing) (off)

"Girl, I love you, tell the world I do-heyyy./
Hope someday you come to love me, too—"

VIRGINIA (off)

Oh, papa . . . help me . . .

The squinting truck driver waddles tentatively into the headlights of the oncoming jalopy.

DISSOLVE.

76. EXTERIOR. HOSPITAL. NIGHT.

The rain has stopped. The panel truck lumbers up to the small hospital. Robert hops off the back. With the driver's assistance he takes Virginia in his arms.

The diminutive stranger steps aside and watches Robert carry Virginia through the lighted door.

77. INTERIOR. HOSPITAL. NIGHT.

Robert paces the floor of the waiting room, his movements catlike and incessant.

The white hospital personnel pass to and fro. A NURSE with a clipboard casually chats with a physician across the floor, pointing toward Robert. She approaches him. He stares at her supplicatingly.

                    NURSE

You the husband?

                    ROBERT

Yes, ma'am.

                    NURSE (writing)

Occupation—

                    ROBERT

Farmer.

                    NURSE (writing)

It was a boy, Johnson. Room two-one-three upstairs.

She turns coldly and exits. Robert follows. She sends him back the opposite way.

78. INTERIOR. HOSPITAL ROOM. NIGHT.

The far window sprays moonlight into the dark, cluttered cell, normally used for equipment and supply storage. Buckets and mops in two corners, a balance scale and two shrouded bodies on mobile stretchers.

Robert steps inside and shuts the door tightly. He looks about the room blankly. He wanders to the first stretcher and peeks under the sheet. He carefully puts the sheet in place again.

He looks about, fixes briefly on the second bed, then gazes upon the darkened window.

Standing before the window, Robert looks behind the curtain, then sets it neatly back in place. He examines the sill, the caulking, the stitching on the cloth.

ROBERT

That was good today, way you took it an' all.
You the type does her cryin' on the inside.

He runs his hand over the far cinder block wall, then along the side wall, approaching the camera. He whistles nervously, almost inaudibly. He pauses.

ROBERT (quietly)

Mmmmm. Her cryin's on the inside.

Robert scans the cell in search of new mysteries. He taps his knuckles on the first stretcher. Silence.

ROBERT

Ain't got no patience for problems, hear? Long
as you in Mississippi you never will get well.
We got work to do, followin' the cotton 'round.
I'm dressin' like a preacher so's we can go from
town to town—

He stands over the second stretcher, moving alongside it
while running his hand lightly over the corpse. His hand
stops at a melon-sized lump between the knees. He
withdraws his hand.

ROBERT

"Chicago." How's that sound—

Robert, his back to the moonlit window, stares down at
the corpse. The rippled, shadowed sheets glow eerily.

ROBERT (hushed)

Virginia?

He stands stiff with fear.

ROBERT (hushed)

Virginia? You goin' with me?

Robert suddenly reaches and pulls the shroud halfway
off. He starts to turn aside, then throws himself onto the
body of beautiful Virginia in a fit of sorrow. The camera
pans outward to the moon.

ROBERT (weeping)

Don't cry, Virginia, don't cry—

DISSOLVE.

79. EXTERIOR. DELTA LANDSCAPE. NIGHT.

SILENT IMAGE: Below the moon the land lies sluggish, a rich expanse of unending blackness. Rounding a bend, a long train rushes through the night, wild sparks flying from its wheels.

The dark, compassionate voice of Blind Willie Johnson moves gently in rhythm with the sequence of images.

RECORDING

"Oh God, God don't never change./ He's God, always will be God—"

The camera pans right, coming upon the misty, cypress-studded Yazoo River.

RECORDING

"God in the middle of the ocean,/ God in the middle of the sea./ By the help of the great Creator—

DISSOLVE.

80. EXTERIOR. RIVERSIDE. DAY.

SILENT IMAGE: A gloomy day. Across the river, a large gathering of mourners in a cypress grove cemetery.

RECORDING

"Truly been a god to me,/ Great God—"

81. EXTERIOR. GRAVEYARD. DAY.

SILENT IMAGE: An emotional throng at Virginia's grave.

Robert kneels dry-eyed in the rabble of tears, as Rev.

Gates pontificates with arms upraised overhead. The
gravedigger is patting down the dirt.

"Oh God, always will be God—"

Sudden tumult at graveside. Hysterical with grief, Hercules pushes people aside while lunging for the grave.
Granville grabs her as Calletta Craft, eyes closed, begins
to faint into Robert's arms.

RECORDING

"God in Creation, God when Adam fell,/ God
way up in heaven—"

Calletta is laid onto the back seat of Granville's car. The
comely woman unconsciously unbuttons her bodice.
Staring at her deathly visage, Robert is startled.

RECORDING

"God way down in hell./ Praise God—"

82.   INTERIOR. TENT. NIGHTFALL.

SILENT IMAGE: Deacon Bates leads the stomping,
shuffling mourners in a delirious "ring shout." Robert
holds his guitar on his lap, seated facing a candlelit
corner.

Calletta, her face tearstained, approaches Robert and
nudges her hip against his shoulder. He looks up, their
eyes meet, she touches his chin with her hand.

RECORDING

"God don't never change./ Oh God, always will
be God—"

DISSOLVE.

83. INTERIOR. BEDROOM. NIGHT.

SILENT IMAGE: Robert lights a white taper in Calletta's pink room. Revealing a most voluptuous body, Calletta sheds her black dress and kneels on the bed, wet eyes beckoning.

RECORDING

"Spoke to the mountain, said how great I am./ Want you up this mornin', skip 'round like a lamb—"

Calletta slips Robert's shirt off his shoulders. The sad woman reclines on her back in the dimness before him, pelvis uplifted, lightly caressing her thighs.

RECORDING

"Well God, God don't ever change./ Ohhhhhhhh, always will be God—"

DISSOLVE.

84. EXTERIOR. LEVEE. BEFORE DAWN.

SILENT IMAGE: Standing against a gray sky atop the flood wall, the lovers are wrapped in each other's arms.

RECORDING

"God in the time of sickness, God in the doctor too,/ In the time of the influenzy, He truly was a god to you—"

85. EXTERIOR. COTTON FIELD. AFTERNOON.

SILENT IMAGE: In brilliant sunlight, Calletta toils to fill her long white sack with cotton. The old recording continues.

86.   INTERIOR. SHACK. AFTERNOON.

SILENT IMAGE: Robert sits listening to a Victrola, waxing his guitar strings with a white candle, drinking whiskey lustily. Calletta's little boys look on unnoticed.

DISSOLVE.

87.   INTERIOR. BEDROOM. NIGHT.

SILENT IMAGE: Robert and Calletta roll on the bed making passionate love in the warm candlelight.

RECORDING

"God in the pulpit, God way down at the door—"

The erotic Calletta takes Robert's hand and presses it onto her large breast. Her lips pursed, her closed eyes are wet with ecstasy.

RECORDING

"It's God in the amen corner, God's all over the floor,/ Praise God—"

Calletta straddles Robert, riding him upright, her hands cupping her breasts.

The voice and guitar fade out. A momentary silence.

Robert's careful, contemplative voice emerges over the sexual imagery, then Calletta's is heard as well. Both voices sound calm, detached, isolated from the other.

ROBERT (off)

I got somethin' to say. A man, like a god, I mean, hisself, through her mouth he got her speech—

CALLETTA (off)

Robert, squeeze my heart, Robert—

88. INTERIOR. BEDROOM. MIDNIGHT.

Calletta is sound asleep. Robert, dressed neatly now, quietly gathers his belongings into a bundle, grabs his guitar and exits.

ROBERT (off)

An', this voice has done me so, as I'll never be my own self again, after I listened, ever since.

CALLETTA (off)

Robert, love me—

89. INTERIOR. KITCHEN. MIDNIGHT.

Robert scoops a handful of pomade from a tin can. Facing the camera as he would a mirror, he slicks his hair back until it is wavy, almost flat.

His appearance altered, Robert takes a large swallow of liquor. He stares searchingly into the camera, unblinking.

90. INTERIOR. BEDROOM. MIDNIGHT.

Through the window we see Robert with guitar and bundle, swigging his bottle, marching off into the night.

Calletta awakens as the sound of his footsteps fades. Seeing that she has been left alone, she rushes inside to the other rooms. She returns and rushes to the window, gazing through her tears at the empty fields.

Little ESAU stands in the doorway rubbing his eye.

ESAU (meekly)

Mama, I got a wind in my belly—

DISSOLVE.

91. INTERIOR. HOSPITAL ROOM. NIGHT.

In the dark cell, Robert leans against the wall beside the window, staring at the moonlit body of Virginia.

ESAU (off)

I got a wind in my belly, Mama—

DISSOLVE.

92. EXTERIOR. JOOK JOINT. NIGHT.

A drunk sits on a stoop outside the overflowing, uproarious jook, savoring a can of Sterno. As he lifts the can to his lips, a couple of JOKERS drop a burning cigarette butt into the fuel. The drunk races off into the woods screaming flames.

JOKERS

CHARLEY PATTON!

SUPER: "Near Lula, Mississippi, 1934"

93. INTERIOR. JOOK JOINT. NIGHT.

An atmosphere of chaotic, simmering violence, with dancing, drinking and gambling in the hazy madhouse.

Charley Patton, his neck swathed in a dirty, blood-soaked rag, sings hoarsely, strenuously, as a perturbed Willie Brown backs him on guitar.

CHARLEY (singing)

"Aw that moon gone down, baby, Clarksdale sun's about to shine./ Rosetta Henry tol' me—"

WILLIE (shouting)

"'Lord, I don't want you hangin' a-round'!'"

CHARLEY (singing)

"Oh, where were you now, baby? Clarksdale mill burned down!"

BULLET WILLIAMS, thoroughly soused, wails away on harp with ROSETTA HENRY hanging all over him. A ruffian named HORSE eyes Rosetta lustily, then glares at Bullet.

CHARLEY (singing) (off)

"There's a house over yonder, painted all over green./ (spoken: Boy, you know I know it's over there)—"

WILLIE (singing)

"Some of the finest young womens, Lord, a man most ever seen—"

Rosetta and the harp-blowing Bullet tumble drunkenly onto Charley, who throws them onto the seated Willie, who then throws them angrily against a wall. Charley gasps, clutching his throat, and keeps singing.

CHARLEY (singing)

"I was evil at midnight when I heard the local blow./ (spoken: Boy, I'm gettin' lonesome)—"

WILLIE (angrily)

Same here, buddy—

Bullet, jostled roughly by annoyed dancers, is pushed down into a chair, with beer poured over his head. Horse glares at him, now moving in. Rosetta retreats, alarmed.

Frustrated, Willie tries to sing as Charley blocks him from the dancers, clowning with his guitar.

WILLIE (singing)

"Oh, the smokestack is black an' the bell it shine like gold—"

CHARLEY (hoarse)

You SHUCKIN', boy! You KNOWS it look GOOD to ME!

WILLIE (rising)

You on yo' own, ol' clown you—

Willie leaves as Charley continues to sing. He passes Horse, who aims a small handgun at the stupefied Bullet with both hands. A thunderous shot. The dancing goes on.

Charley and others hit the deck as Bullet stares upward at Horse, the blues harp in his hands, sitting calmly.

ROSETTA

Bullet! You dead!

BULLET

Naw, I ain't dead.

HORSE (blows on gun)

Huh.

Bullet rises nonchalantly and walks into the kitchen. Charley, on his back, continues to sing.

CHARLEY (singing)

"Gonna move to Alabama, graveyard to be your home—"

The wild dancing, drinking, sex and gambling resume.

94. EXTERIOR. GRAVEL ROAD. NIGHT.

Robert walks through the opaque stillness wearing a hat, a dark suit and white shirt without tie, with his guitar slung over onto his back. He carries his customary whiskey bottle.

Willie, walking in the opposite direction, passes Robert by without recognizing him. He also carries a bottle.

ROBERT

Say, Willie Brown.

WILLIE (stopping)

Who that—

ROBERT (drinking)

Now who you think?

WILLIE

Goodness sakes: Little Robert. Let me take a look at you. Where you been? It's well-nigh—

ROBERT

Coupla years now maybe. Been all over, man. All over. Playin' an' makin' my move, y'know. Gettin' my licks.

WILLIE (drinking)

Look like you been to the moon. Hmm—what's
that on your eye?

Closeup of Robert. An odd, opaque white dot covers
part of his left eye.

ROBERT

Aw, nothin' much, been gettin' it from time to
time.

WILLIE

One of them eclipses.

ROBERT (drinking)

Yeah. All of them womens, likely.

WILLIE

See you got your gui-tar. Charley's playin' over
yonder jook, singin' like a dog. Bertha Lee's cut
his throat pretty good.

ROBERT (drinking)

Yeah. Heard she singin' with him still.

WILLIE (drinking)

Oh, they in love, but he's alone tonight. He's
ready for you. You go take that motherfucker
now—

Each pats the other's shoulder as they part.

95. INTERIOR. JOOK JOINT. NIGHT.

Charley, straining mightily, sings amid the dancing mob in the dimly lit shack, constantly sucking on a whiskey bottle to wet his throat.

CHARLEY (singing)

"I got me a stone pony, don't ride Shetlands no more./ You can find my stone pony hooked to my rider's door—"

To the side, Bullet is drinking hootch with a grotesque crimson splotch on his chest. Charley sings behind him.

ROSETTA

Bullet, you here drinkin' still? Don't you know you been shot?

BULLET

Naw, I ain't shot.

ROSETTA

Oh yes you is, Bull. Now I'm gonna get yo' hat, so you get out 'fore ol' Horse come back an' kill you sure enough.

BULLET

All right. You want me to go.

Rosetta puts the hat on his head. Bottle in hand, Bullet goes through the door, steps into the yard outside and drops dead. We see Robert turn from the hootch table, step over Bullet's body and enter the jook.

CHARLEY (singing)

"I got me a stone pony, don't ride Shetlands no more./ You can find my stone pony hooked to my rider's door—"

Robert pushes through the dancers and stands in the corner, playing his guitar behind Charley, who looks over his shoulder at him. When Charley finishes the next verse, Robert steps forward and challenges.

CHARLEY (singing)

"Well, I didn't come here to steal nobody's brown,/ Just stopped by here to keep you from stealin' mine!"

ROBERT (singing)

"Hello, Central, what's the matter with your line?/ Come a storm last night an' tore the wire down!"

CHARLEY (singing)

"Vicksburg on a high hill, an' Natchez down below,/ An' I don't feel welcome, man, no matter where I go—"

VOICES

Charley! Stay with 'im! Shout it!

ROBERT (singing)

"Vicksburg on a high hill, mama, Natchez far below,/ Goin' back home, mama, to the Gulf of Mexico!"

VOICES

Go! Stranger! Play it!

A great singing duel is being waged. Charley, older than Robert by twenty years, fights hard. Robert, more intense, is brilliantly rousing. A dizzying rhythm.

The crowd urges Charley on with coins and booze. Robert throws his hat away, and Charley tries blocking him from the dancers. Robert turns to the wall, smiling.

CHARLEY (singing)

"Ain't got no job, mama, rollin' through this world./ When I leave now, mama, goin' further down the road—"

VOICES

Stay, Charley! Cut 'im, Charley!

ROBERT (singing)

"Said when I leave here, mama, goin' further down the road/ An' if I get back here ain't gonna never be bad no mo'—"

Robert turns around again to find Charley clutching his throat and gagging. But he improvises yet another verse.

CHARLEY (singing)

"An' my baby got a heart like a piece of railroad steel/ An'—"

Charley gasps. Clowning no more, he struggles to go on.

ROBERT

Sit down, Charley—

CHARLEY (singing)

"My baby got—"

ROBERT

I got you, Charley, time to sit down—

103

CHARLEY (singing)

"—got a heart of railroad steel/ An' if I leave here this mornin' don't say, 'Daddy, how you feel?'—"

Charley starts to choke and rushes unnoticed out of the jook. Robert, strange-looking with his straight hair and bad eye, shouts on in the maelstrom, alone.

DISSOLVE.

96. INTERIOR. JOOK JOINT. MIDNIGHT.

The jook is at its most feverish pitch. Robert sings his supreme dance number, "Walkin' Blues."

ROBERT (singing)

"I woke up this mornin', feelin' 'round for my shoes./ Ooo-now, got these, ol' walkin' blues—"

VOICES

Shout it! Truth! Sing it! Work it!

A stocky, jet-black youth with a harmonica in hand is studying Robert's dazzling guitar work. Robert sees him and, nervously running his fingers through his hair, he turns away and goes on singing.

ROBERT (singing)

"Lord, I feel like blowin' my ol' lonesome home./ Got up this mornin' my lil Calletta's gone, well—"

A wench dances seductively for Robert as another woman puts money in his guitar. Performing to them, Robert sees the youth eyeing him beyond.

ROBERT (singing)

"Well, I leave this morn' if I have to woh! oh,
ride the blinds./ I been mistreated an' I don'
mind dyin'—"

The youth stares fixedly at Robert's hands. As the crowd
dances with dizzy momentum, Robert slips away. No
one in the jook misses a step, even without music.

97. EXTERIOR. COTTON FIELD. MIDNIGHT.

Walking with guitar in tow, Robert hears a coughing
and gagging sound somewhere amid the stalks. At first
fearful, Robert is relieved to see Charley stagger into
view, clutching his bandaged throat. Upon seeing Robert, Charley puts on a brave act.

CHARLEY

I'll kill 'em all, those charlies. I'll git 'em, I'll
bust 'em up—

ROBERT

Who you foolin', man—

CHARLEY

Jus' lookin' to whup some pink ass. So happy I
could shout an' *shit*—

He starts gagging and choking frightfully.

ROBERT

I'm headin' 'cross this field to that jook over
yonder. C'mon with me, man; how 'bout it, le's
go—

CHARLEY

Can't. Gotta get to Holly Ridge 'fore Bertha Lee starts to flay me again. . . . Next time.

Robert shrugs and walks on, but stops when Charley gags again. He gasps for air. A grotesque pathos.

ROBERT

You the best ever was, Charley Patton. Best ever was—

Charley stands on buckling knees in the cotton field, watching Robert trek onward to the faraway jook. Behind Charley, in the first jook, the patrons are filtering out in search of their musicians.

VOICES (distant)

Stranger, play! Charley! Where ol' Charley? Charley! Come back—

He trudges back.

98. INTERIOR. ROADSIDE JOOK. WEE HOURS.

Robert is seated in the overcrowded den, proceeding powerfully with "Walkin' Blues." Liquor is everywhere.

ROBERT (singing)

"Well! Some people tell me that the worried blues ain't bad./ Worst ol' feelin' I most e-ver had—"

A sexy woman dances in front of him, holding her skirt hem higher and higher on her thigh.

ROBERT (singing)

"She's got Elgin movements from her head
down to her toes,/ Break in on a dollar most
anywhere she goes—"

She shakes her shapely ass in Robert's face. Her angry
boyfriend looks on as Robert kisses it tenderly.

99. EXTERIOR. ROADSIDE JOOK. WEE HOURS.

The teeming, ramshackle café is set upon from all sides
by sharecroppers in cars, wagons and on foot.

ROBERT (singing) (off)

"Ooooooooooooooooooo!/ From her head down to
her toes—"

A drunken man with his shirt unbuttoned bursts out of
the jook smiling wide, arms upraised triumphantly.

DISSOLVE.

100. EXTERIOR. FRIARS POINT. NOON.

A massive throng swarms upon Hirsberg's Drugstore,
dancing, clapping, laughing, as Robert generates a strong
primal rhythm with his guitar and ringing voice.

ROBERT (singing)

"Ohhhh! Baby don't you want to go?/ Back to
the land of California, to my sweet home, Chicago?"

The white drugstore owner taps his foot and whistles
while counting a thick roll of dollar bills in the doorway.
Folks enter and exit his store nonstop.

The crowd showers Robert with coins and encouragement. Robert notices the jet-black youth seen earlier, again staring hard at Robert's amazingly fast hands.

ROBERT (singing)

"Now two an' two is four, four an' two is six./ Keep monkeyin' 'round here, friendboy, you get yo' business all in tricks—"

DISSOLVE.

101. EXTERIOR. FRIARS POINT. LATE AFTERNOON.

The enormous crowd now carouses in an empty grass lot as Robert shouts his song over a driving guitar rhythm.

ROBERT (singing)

"I got ramblin', I've got ramblin' on my mind./ I got mean things, I've got mean things on my mind—"

White policemen are setting up roadblocks as the dancing mob grows ever larger. Beer-drinking rednecks are stomping to the beat on nearby rooftops.

ROBERT (singing)

"Runnin' down to the station, catch the first mail train I see./ Got the blues 'bout Miss So-an'-so, an' the child's got the blues about me—"

A crotchety old redneck pours his beer on the throng from above.

DISSOLVE.

102. EXTERIOR. HOUSE PARTY. NIGHT.

At least two hundred black people are in and around a shack on a gravel road in a cotton field. Jalopies and wagons cart them from miles around to hear Robert.

ROBERT (singing) (off)

"If your man gets personal, won't you have your fun./ Jus' come on back to Friars Point, mama, barrelhouse all night long—"

103. INTERIOR. HOUSE PARTY. NIGHT.

A beautiful slow boogie, the song has a hypnotic effect on the dancers. The simple wood shack is so packed that the walls bulge and the dangling light bulb flickers, as bodies rub to the sensuous rhythm. Robert, seated, is being caressed by several women at once amid the shaking crush.

ROBERT (singing)

"Now you can squeeze my lemon till the juice run down my— (spoken: You know what I'm talkin' 'bout—)

"You can squeeze my lemon till the juice run down my bed./ (spoken: That's what I'm talkin' 'bout now—)"

A dense mass of stomping feet pounds the wooden floor.

104. EXTERIOR. HOUSE PARTY. NIGHT.

From afar we observe the swaying shack, the dancers in the flickering light, the drinking scene outside.

ROBERT (singing) (off)

"But I'm goin' back to Friars Point if I be rockin' to my head—"

As if in SLOW MOTION, the floor inside caves in. We hear a mixture of shrieks and laughter.

FADE OUT.

105. EXTERIOR. COTTON FIELD AND ROAD. MORNING.

FADE IN.

Men and women labor in the awful heat. A man hollers a melodic plaint.

> FIELD HOLLERER

"Don't know what in this world I gonna do, oh, mama,/ Don't know what in this world I gonna do—"

The mournful singer hears the distant drone of an airplane. He stuffs his sack with a cotton boll, then he shields his eyes, searching the blinding skies.

106. EXTERIOR. GRAVEL ROAD. MORNING.

Marching along a sweeping bend beside the field, Robert hears the oncoming rumble of the plane and looks upward. He is dressed neatly in brand-new striped pants with suspenders, two-toned shoes, white shirt and panama hat.

As Robert lifts his ever present bottle to his lips, a gleefully plastered Goat passes by on a wobbly bicycle and swipes the bottle deftly. Immediately, the airplane roars down from above with jarring suddenness.

Goat, drinking, rides his bike into a ditch, as hundreds of white sheets of paper flutter and fall from the sky. Robert laughs at Goat and walks ahead, grabbing a page out of the air and reading it.

FLIER

THE DEATH OF CHARLEY PATTON!
Poor ol' Charley Patton's had one "Spoonful"
too many, so now we see him leave his "Pony
Blues" behind as he goes "Down the Dirt
Road" where the "High Sheriff" and "Revenue
Man" can't find him. Buy Charley's last great
hit "POOR ME" at your best bet, POWELL'S MUSIC
in Jackson TODAY!"

Staring at the page, Robert's pace quickens to a run.

107. EXTERIOR. COTTON FIELD. MORNING.

The hollerer looks up from the advertisement. As the
small plane loops and spins acrobatically in another
field, a police car stops. Two white cops lasso Goat, drag
him roughly from the ditch and throw him inside the
car.

108. EXTERIOR. LULA. AFTERNOON.

The tiny railroad town is thronged by hundreds of black
people mourning the death of Charley Patton. A loud,
compelling African drumming shakes the air.

In the center of town, by the railroad tracks, a strange
and exciting event: two youths dance madly atop a covered flatbed wagon playing "The Devil's Dream" on fife
and bass drum. The massive gathering bumps and
grinds to the mesmerizing tribal rhythm.

Atop the wagon, propped upright in an open casket behind the performers, the body of Charley Patton looks
on.

Robert stands on the edge of the crowd drinking whiskey while watching the amazing performance. He sees
the REV. SIN-KILLER GRIFFIN climb onto the platform with

a megaphone and, waving his arms, command the crowd's attention. Robert wanders toward a nearby bar.

SIN-KILLER

Brothers and sisters, our subject in this lamentable hour: "There's Nothin' to Do in HELL"!

VOICES

All right! Come on now!

SIN-KILLER

You know, it look to me like your ol' preacher Sin-Killer here sees lotsa folks jus' wanna go to HELL!

VOICES

Yessuh! Tell me 'bout it!

SIN-KILLER

But I prefer goin' the OTHER way! I been told there was a sin SELLER said he jus' didn't want NO heaven, that he was wantin' to go to HELL!

VOICES (singing)

Ohhhhhhhhhhh yeahhhhhhhhhhhhhhhhh—

Grinning slightly, the dead Charley Patton stands back of the ranting preacher.

109.   INTERIOR. LULA BAR. AFTERNOON.

Robert guzzles a pint of whiskey in the doorway.

SIN-KILLER (off)

Asked WHY, the sin SELLER said, "Well, there's too much to DO in heaven! Every mornin' you

got to put out the MOON, an' then the STARS, an'
then hang out the SUN!" Said he'd rather go to
HELL an' do NOTHIN' but keep his FEETS to the
FIRE!

VOICES (off)

A-MENNNNNNNN—

An atmosphere of drunken sorrow in the dingy joint. A
jukebox plays Charley Patton's "Poor Me" as the patrons
drink and moan.

JUKEBOX (off)

"It's on me, poor me, you must have pity on
poor me./ I ain't got nobody, take pity on poor
me—"

Robert stands at the bar gulping down a fresh bottle of
whiskey. The fifer and bass drummer enter. They slap
down change and take their bottles to a table. Robert
eyes them as an OLD DRUNK eyes him.

OLD DRUNK

I can line ninety-eight whores up against a wall,
an' I'll bet you a quarter I can fuck 'em all—

Ignoring him, drunken Robert feels his way to the musicians' table. Drinking heavily, the three men huddle together, talking low and serious. A sexy woman stands
over Robert. Ignored, she walks away.

OLD DRUNK (off)

Hey, baby—shiiiiiiit. . . .

110. EXTERIOR. LULA. LATE AFTERNOON.

The crowd is chanting feverishly as the preacher tries to
quiet them for the spinsterly MOTHER MC COLLUM.

CROWD (singing)

"Hell is a miserable place, I'm told./ It got no peace an' quiet, it got no one alive—"

SIN-KILLER

Brothers! Sisters! Mother McCollum's here to—

CROWD (singing)

"Hell is a miserable place, I'm told!"

Vigorously strumming her big guitar, Mother McCollum momentarily distracts the crowd by bursting into song.

MOTHER M. (singing)

"Oh, Jesus is my air-o-plane./ He rides over us all, He don't ever fall./ Jesus is my air-o-plane—"

As the beatific old black woman strains to sing over the raucous din, Sin-Killer climbs down from the wagon and heads for the bar.

In the distance, Sin-Killer comes upon the fifer and bass drummer, who lead Robert by the arm like a blind man. The preacher blesses poor Robert and rushes on.

111. EXTERIOR. ATOP WAGON. LATE AFTERNOON.

Beneath the overhang, flies and ants congregate about the oily face of Charley Patton. The song continues above the tumult.

"Blind" Robert Johnson is helped onto the wagon, then into a chair with his guitar. He faces forward quietly.

MOTHER M. (singing)

"Jesus is COMIN' in His AIR-o-plane!"

The woman bows to the boisterous assembly, smiling sweetly at Charley, then at Robert, while climbing off. "Blind" Robert smiles sweetly back. So does Charley.

Suddenly Robert stares outward, back erect, his foot stomping hard on the wood.

Hooting excitedly, the crowd immediately picks up the beat.

112. INTERIOR. LULA BAR. LATE AFTERNOON.

A loud, pounding rhythm is swelling up outside.

> JUKEBOX (off)
>
> "Don't the moon look pretty shinin' down through the tree./ I can see Bertha Lee, but she can't see me—"

Drunken Sin-Killer takes his bottle and turns for the door. The thundering rhythm intensifies.

> BARTENDER

Say! Reverend! Damn. Never pays.

Now a lively guitar heightens the deafening momentum beyond. The preacher hurriedly exits.

113. EXTERIOR. ATOP WAGON. LATE AFTERNOON.

His shiny knife flashing over the guitar strings, Robert shouts his ringing song to the roused mob.

> ROBERT (singing)
>
> "If I HAD POSSESSION, over JUDGMENT DAY/ The womens I'm LOVIN' wouldn't have no RIGHT to PRAY!"

Sin-Killer pushes through the dancers for the wagon.

ROBERT (singing)

"An' I went to the MOUNTAIN, lookin' FAR as my
EYES could SEE—"

The preacher climbs clumsily onto the wagon and waves
his arms wildly, now grabbing his bullhorn, shouting.

Robert stands and, no longer blind, his foot stomping
hard, he faces Charley Patton, performing electrically,
energy raving madly.

ROBERT (singing)

"I ROLLED an' I TUMBLED an' I CRIED THE WHOLE
NIGHT LONG./ Boy I woke up this mornin', my
BEST FRIEND CHARLEY—GONE!"

On cue, the big bass drum suddenly erupts, pounding
out the beat ferociously, as the fifer and drummer incite
the throng into an awesome tribal dance-chant. Instinc-
tively the crowd moves with it.

FIFER, DRUMMER

CHARLEY PATTON DEAD AN' GONE, LEFT ME HERE
TO WEEP AN' MOAN/ OHHHH—

His feet stomping to the irresistible beat, Sin-Killer rants
through his megaphone, his words lost in the uproarious
chanting.

SIN-KILLER

I SAY TO YOU, WHEN HE COME DOWN HIS HAIR
GONNA BE LIKE LAMB'S WOOL! AN' HIS EYES LIKE

FLAMES O' FIRE! AN' EVERY MAN KNOW HE THE
SON OF THE TRUE LIVIN' GOD—

MASS CHANT

CHARLEY PATTON DEAD AN' GONE, LEFT ME HERE
TO WEEP AN' MOAN/ OHHHHH—

114. EXTERIOR. LULA. TWILIGHT.

From the edge of the riotous scene we see Robert facing
the upright casket, dancing, playing guitar, as the mani-
acal preacher dances himself, shouting vainly. A plane
drones overhead.

MASS CHANT

CHARLEY PATTON DEAD AN' GONE, LEFT ME HERE
TO WEEP AN' MOAN/ OHHHH—

SIN-KILLER

AN' HE GONNA HAVE A TREE BEFORE THE TWELVE
MANNERS OF FOOD! AN' THE LEAVES TO BE HEALIN'
DAMNATION! AN' THE BIG RACIAL ROCK THAT YOU
CAN SET BEHIND, THE WIND CAN'T BLOW AT YOU NO
MORE—

A few white cops are seen eyeing the mob. Robert and
the preacher dance atop the wagon with others now.
The people are beating anything vibrant: oil drums,
chairs, tree trunks. The flood of rhythm is monstrous. We
hear the plane swooping low.

MASS CHANT

CHARLEY PATTON DEAD AN' GONE, OHHH—

A shower of fluttering sheets of paper descends with the
darkness. Surging bedlam. The body of Charley Patton
looks on.

FAST DISSOLVE.

115. EXTERIOR. GRAVEL ROAD. NIGHT.

Robert whistles to himself while walking along the road. Off camera we hear another pounding drumbeat, this time wedded to an old fifer's waltz, "After the Ball Is Over."

A police car overtakes Robert and pulls over. Before the strange waltz can fade out, two white cops hop out and drag Robert roughly behind some bushes.

Beaten, Robert slumps to the ground. One COP kneels over the slender victim as the second COP examines the guitar.

COP 1

Yeah, got a bad eye. It's him.

COP 2

Mmm, a Gibson, musta stole it. Say, should I do this gui-tar?

SIN-KILLER (off)

Fellas! Wait! Have mercy!

A car door slams as the preacher rushes over. The cops return to their vehicle. Sin-Killer stands over Robert, lying flat in a mess of fallen white fliers.

SIN-KILLER

The moral's yours, because it's mine. This'll teach you—

Robert struggles to sit up, holding his stomach.

SIN-KILLER (off)

—good.

He exits. Robert, bloodied, reaches for his guitar.

116. EXTERIOR. SHACK. NIGHT.

The shack is dark but for a corner, candlelit window. Robert trudges into view, goes to the window and peers inside. Looking unkempt, his face is somehow unmarked.

Standing naked before a mirror in the dim pink room, Calletta massages her magnificent body sensuously with a thick oil. We hear Robert quietly enter the shack.

ROBERT (off)

Calletta? You still want me?

Startled, Calletta sees Robert step into her room.

CALLETTA (sobbing)

Robert, my God, oh Robert—

She embraces him, burying his face in her breasts. They descend to the bed. She snuffs out the candle. Sounds of breathless ecstasy.

FADE OUT.

117. INTERIOR. BEDROOM. NIGHT.

FADE IN.

Darkness. Silence. Then the bodies shift in the bed.

ROBERT (hushed)

It's on me, Calletta. Me. All fear. Nervous over what's goin' on. Calletta?

CALLETTA (sleepy)

Mmmmmmmmm—

ROBERT (hushed)

Like I'm between two dangers, of where I sleep an' where I start. Not knowin' what's less hurt, what'll kill the fastest, got me worryin' all 'bout it. Got me into a life I don't really understand myself—a bad life. Me an' my friends, we fool around, they can't help me an' I can't help them.

CALLETTA (hushed)

Robert, marry me.

A momentary lull.

ROBERT (hushed)

Don't know quite what I'm goin' to do 'bout it. Had a dream before: I was a little boy walkin', lookin' for his father—

FADE OUT.

118. INTERIOR. COURTHOUSE. AFTERNOON.

FADE IN.

An ordinary office with pale green cinder block walls. Robert has shaved his head bald. Writing slowly, he is signing a marriage certificate. As Calletta bends over to sign, he puts on his hat and exits.

Surprised to see Robert gone, she smiles awkwardly at the white justice of the peace.

119. EXTERIOR. COURTHOUSE STEPS. AFTERNOON.

Looking about, Robert fixes his eye on a white fellow staring at his wristwatch. Robert starts toward him, then turns to a black FARMER ascending the steps.

ROBERT

Say, what time you got?

Smirking slightly, the farmer points sunward.

FARMER

Long 'bout . . . half past two.

Calletta joins Robert and they walk down the steps.

ROBERT

Now we gonna keep this secret, hear? You can have your party, but this gotta be a secret. No one's s'posed to know—

120. INTERIOR. SHACK. AFTERNOON.

Robert sits alone in a corner by the Victrola, picking at his guitar, humming "Come On in My Kitchen." Outside, the singsong chatter of children at play.

Calletta's little boy JOE dashes across the room and out the door. Esau, rubbing his eye and holding a book, stumbles out after him.

ESAU

Joe? Mama?

121. EXTERIOR. SHACK. AFTERNOON.

Separate groups of four little girls and four little boys bounce about gleefully, clapping their hands to a rhythm. Joe plays; Esau rubs his eye, book in hand.

Smiling, Calletta stands nearby at a kettle of boiling water over a fire, doing a wash. She picks up her long wood staff and jabs the water.

GIRLS (off)

"Steal up, you boys, don't slight us none/ 'Cause them you slight won't have no fun!"

BOYS (off)

"Hey satisfied! Hey satisfied!—"

Still rubbing his eye, Esau walks over to his mother. He points to a caterpillar crawling up her staff.

ESAU

Mama!

CALLETTA

A baby caterpillar, Esau!

Esau nudges it onto his open book. CLOSEUP of the long, wormlike insect larva crawling over the illustrated, text-printed page.

ESAU (off)

Does he know anything?

CALLETTA (off)

He knows some simple tasks an' things—

ESAU (off)

He still gonna know it when he's a butterfly?

CALLETTA (off)

No, Esau—once he gets his wings he'll forget.

ESAU

When I get my wings will I forget?

CALLETTA

Not if you an angel. Angels don't never forget.

The boys and girls jump up and down together now in a circle, around a cute little girl in the middle.

BOYS

"See that girl with the red dress on?/ She gonna buck-dance all night long!"

GIRLS

"Hey satisfied! Hey satisfied!"

Robert exits the shack with his guitar. As Calletta jabs her staff into the water he kisses her and moves on.

CALLETTA (smiling)

Hey! When you gettin' ready?

ROBERT

I'm ready. Jus' takin' a walk now. Remember: it's a secret—

CALLETTA

Party's startin' at eight! I'm gonna look good enough to eat!

ROBERT

You better be waitin' on me!

She dips the staff back into the water and holds aloft a pair of Robert's striped trousers.

CHILDREN (off)

"Hey satisfied! Hey satisfied!"

Robert treks down the small road toward the levee.

122. EXTERIOR. LEVEE. TWILIGHT.

The skies are ablaze with the setting sun as Robert marches head down atop the dark green flood wall.

123. INTERIOR. BEDROOM. TWILIGHT.

Calletta enters the room wearing a white bathrobe and a white towel, wrapped like a turban, on her head. She carefully lays her red party dress on the bed. She sits down, removes the towel, starts combing her wet hair.

Calletta rises and moves toward the camera, standing in front of the mirror, still combing her shiny hair. She slips off her robe. Gazing steadily at the mirror, Calletta dabs her skin with perfumed scent, first the throat, the breasts, then the buttocks and groin, delicately.

She picks up her red dress and holds it over her body, assessing herself in the mirror.

DISSOLVE.

124. INTERIOR. BEDROOM. NIGHTFALL.

Standing before the mirror, Calletta is transformed by her tight red dress, her earrings, her painted lips and cheeks.

The boys walk in wearing party suits. Smiling adoringly, she stoops and fixes Esau's bow tie.

125. EXTERIOR. RIVERSIDE CAMP. NIGHTFALL.

The canvas tent flaps and billows, the hanging lanterns sway and throw bizarre shadows. A windy night sets in.

Robert approaches on the dirt road, strumming his guitar carefully, lifting it to his ear while walking. He proceeds further toward the river.

A muscular worker rubs his girlfriend's posterior while swigging his whiskey bottle, walking her into the dark woods.

126. EXTERIOR. RIVERSIDE. NIGHTFALL.

Robert passes a small herd of cows feeding on tall grass near the river. He sits down on a tiny ridge and huddles over his guitar, picking and humming to himself.

In the foreground, among the cows, an empty rowboat. The herdsman JOHNNY SHINES—the stocky, jet-black youth seen earlier fixed on Robert's guitar work—sits with a bottle in the boat.

Robert, his hat off, looks strange with his bad eye and clean-shaven head. He sings to himself now, quietly.

ROBERT (singing)

"Oh oh she gone, I know she won't come back./
I taken her last nickel, out her nation sack./

You better come on, hmmmmm hmmmmm
hmm hmm,/ It's gonna be rainin' outdoors—"

Johnny hears the gentle song and stands, turning
around. Robert continues playing with a spoken passage, his guitar trembling like the nervous air. He does
not notice Johnny yet, gazing from behind some bushes.

ROBERT (spoken)

"(Baby, can't you hear the wind howl./ Oh,
how the wind do howl—)"

Robert sees Johnny. He takes his hat and guitar and
starts walking farther up the riverside. Johnny calls,
"Hey!" and catches up with him.

ROBERT (stern)

Third time, man—I don't like it.

He walks past Johnny toward the moaning cows. Johnny
catches up again. They stop to talk.

JOHNNY

I ain't tryin' to cut you. I can't do that, I seen
you play—you the man of the day. What you
doin' here 'round Lula, Friars Point anyway?
I'm John, Shines—

He takes a hit of liquor and passes the bottle to Robert.

ROBERT (drinking)

What you think I'm doin' here?

JOHNNY

Money? Hell, it's all over in Arkansas. West
Helena, man, over yonder—

126

Drinking, the two men stare across the Mississippi River. The cows moan in the windy darkness behind them.

127.   INTERIOR. SHACK. NIGHT.

Calletta rushes about, setting food and drinks on the table, them selecting a record for the Victrola. Footsteps outside; she opens the door expectantly.

A black couple hugs Calletta joyfully. She smiles politely as they enter, then she steps into the night air.

128.   EXTERIOR. BOAT ON RIVER. NIGHT.

His back to the bow, Johnny rows away from shore. Robert sits opposite him, drinking.

JOHNNY (quietly)

West Helena's got the best musicianers any-where, man. Sonny Boy Williamson's there, Peetie Wheatstraw sometimes, Kokomo Arnold the same, Buddy Boy Hawkins, a big kid named Chester, calls hisself "Howlin' Wolf"—these ain't some drunken niggers jookin' in a field, man. You find record jobbers lookin' in, a white guy, name of Oertle. You go there, join a record company, hell; make some of that money—

Robert drinks up. The cows moan on the shore behind as the little skiff moves over the silent black water. A beautiful wild duck paddles up, following alongside.

Johnny keeps rowing, the bottle goes back and forth. Floating down the middle of the river, a covered barge looms distantly. Robert and Johnny talk quietly.

ROBERT

What's comin'?

JOHNNY

Can't tell.

The barge drifts closer. We hear laughing female voices.
Groups of dark figures on deck become discernible.

ROBERT (hushed)

Womens—

JOHNNY (hushed)

It's the *Katy Adams*—

Johnny rows feverishly, trying to intersect the distant
barge's path, the duck quacking behind. Eighty yards
ahead, the covered barge floats slowly by. Johnny quits
rowing. Robert stares hard.

Standing on deck, painted black wenches are chattering,
laughing, searching the shoreline. As the rowboat drifts
closer, a few women pass by pointing gleefully. Three of
them lift their skirts and jiggle the sack of shiny gold
coins each has hanging between her thighs. A black
man with a shotgun is steering in a crowd at the stern.
Sad Virginia moves helplessly along the bottom edge.

JOHNNY (hushed) (off)

The Memphis whores, goin' down to Rosedale,
man—

WHORE

Ooo! Hey! Pretty boy! Want it!

Robert holds his hat as the barge exits into darkness.
Virginia disappears last. The duck quacks once.

129. EXTERIOR. ARKANSAS SHORE. NIGHT.

The dark water slaps against the side of the boat as it
drifts ashore. Johnny hops off and pulls it out of the
water. Robert stands in the skiff, holding two guitars.
Floating silently, the duck looks on.

> ROBERT
>
> Pay you later.

> JOHNNY
>
> Yeah, man.

> ROBERT (stepping off)
>
> You goin' with me?

> JOHNNY
>
> Stop an' get my cousin Calvin, drive us the rest
> of the way.

Johnny turns the boat over. He throws a fishing net over
it, then covers it with leaves and weed. Robert and
Johnny exit with their guitars.

130. EXTERIOR. RISING SUN CAFÉ. NIGHT.

Hand-painted letters on the cracked pane: RISING SUN
CAFÉ. To the right, below, crudely scrawled: "more
than just a Bar." A sign in the window: "tamales." We
hear a wild jug band inside wreaking gay delirium.

> STREET VENDOR (off)
>
> Dead shrimmmmp, shrimp man out here—

The gentle vendor pushes his cart through a talkative
throng of well-dressed black men and women, milling in

the street and on the sidewalk, drinking. A white Terraplane convertible emblazoned with "TAMPA RED'S HOKUM BAND!" is parked at the curb.

131. INTERIOR. RISING SUN CAFÉ. NIGHT.

Exposed dangling light bulbs with cardboard reflectors swing and flicker in the commotive joint. On the corner bandstand the great singer and female impersonator FRANKIE JAXON dances and struts histrionically, now mocking a bug-eyed sideman blowing on a huge glass jug. He sings with a woman's voice, dressed in a white vest, gloves and black pants, like a fancy hotel attendant.

FRANKIE (singing)

"Ooo, baby! Tight like that!/ I mean, it's tight like that!/ In the morn' it's tight like that!/ In the alley now, tight like that!—"

In a baggy suit, red beret and string tie, dumpy TAMPA RED slides his steel guitar, a kazoo tooting between his lips, leading his band like a young black Lawrence Welk. Tall, handsome GEORGIA TOM, acting very cool in his fur coat and felt hat cocked over one eye, carries a brandy snifter through the dancers to his piano.

FRANKIE (to Tom)

If you can't sell it, sit on it!

Tom takes his cue and pounds the keys spectacularly.

FRANKIE (singing)

"C'mon, boy, jive that thing!/ Git to me, tight like that!/ That's it! Boot it! You ain't no mama's child!"

Little Frankie flies over the hot piano.

132.   INTERIOR. JALOPY. NIGHT.

Young CALVIN FRAZIER drives with Johnny beside him.
Robert is in the back seat drinking, picking his guitar.

JOHNNY

You need an agent, man. I'll be your agent.

CALVIN

Hacksaw, he put them guys in the shade once.
He got an agent.

ROBERT

I don't need no agent. This white guy you
talkin' 'bout, he jus' be standin' there, see.

CALVIN

Say, man, what name you gonna be?

133.   EXTERIOR. JALOPY ON RIVER ROAD. NIGHT.

The jalopy sputters along beside the immense river.

JOHNNY (off)

Sudan Washington—

ROBERT (off)

Robert Johnson.

CALVIN (off)

Somethin' original—

We are left staring across the dark water at Mississippi.

134. INTERIOR. RISING SUN CAFÉ. NIGHT.

With crocodile tears wetting his face and gloves, Frankie Jaxon mournfully mocks a popular blues number.

FRANKIE (singing)

"How long . . . how long . . . how long, daddy, how long?/ How long . . . how long . . . ooo, howww long—"

135. EXTERIOR. RISING SUN CAFÉ. NIGHT.

Calvin parks the jalopy beside the white convertible. The three young men enter with their guitars.

136. INTERIOR. SHACK. NIGHT.

In Calletta's candlelit main room, a somber house party. Drunken dancers step dreadfully slow to a jazz record on the Victrola. Calletta, painfully unhappy, lets her eyes wander out a side window.

137. INTERIOR. RISING SUN CAFÉ. NIGHT.

Crawling now on his hands and knees, Frankie sings to the jug blower, then he moves toward Tampa Red.

FRANKIE (singing)

"How long . . . how long . . . how long?/ Oh, jump me now! How longggg—"

Standing by the wall looking on, wearing a wrinkled shirt with rolled-up sleeves and tie, the white talent scout ERNIE OERTLE sips a beer.

Seen through drifting figures at the bar, drinking a pint of whiskey, Robert spots Oertle and eyes him fixedly. Oertle finds a table near the bandstand.

FRANKIE

"Oh, Mr. Tampa, you must be a Florida man!"

Frankie, on his knees, is stroking Tampa Red's leg to the music. Tampa starts gasping through his kazoo.

Standing over Oertle now in tattered suit and hat, unkempt BUDDY BOY HAWKINS seems to be pleading with the talent scout, who shakes his head and watches Frankie shine. Pathetic Buddy Boy persists.

At the bar, Johnny is nudging the transfixed Robert, who sips his whiskey and strokes his guitar. As he observes Oertle we hear Robert's imaginary dialogue between the voice of Clark Gable-as-Oertle and himself.

ROBERT (off)

Excuse me, sir—you the man that makes them records?

GABLE-OERTLE (off)

Yeah, for a few guys, sometimes. Why do you ask, young fella?

ROBERT (off)

On account of—I'm Robert Johnson. One of the famous Johnson boys.

GABLE-OERTLE (off)

Robert Johnson, Robert Johnson—

ROBERT (off)

Robert Lonnie Johnson.

GABLE-OERTLE (off)

No, don't reckon I—

ROBERT (off)

I got other names, like Dodds, or then I can be
Spencer, in certain places I can be Robert
Spencer, as Robert Johnson ain't my only name,
necessarily—

Oertle is annoyed with Buddy Boy and sends him away.
Johnny moves through the crowd and approaches Oertle, urgently talking to him. Buddy Boy lingers desperately.

ROBERT (off)

"Terrible Slug"—I can be that too.

GABLE-OERTLE (off)

What do you play?

ROBERT (off)

Everything, on gui-tar. Like Duke Ellington,
Blind Lemon, Kokomo, all of the music. Bing
Crosby, Leroy Carr—

As Johnny points at Robert, Oertle stands and heads for
the bar. We study the dreamlost Robert close up.

GABLE-OERTLE (off)

You sing?

ROBERT (off)

Dance, too.

GABLE-OERTLE (off)

Don't care about that.

ROBERT (off)

I sing better than whatever you can name, any ol' kind o' tangled-up music you like. I'm it.

OERTLE

You Robert Johnson?

Robert, startled out of his fantasy, finds himself facing Ernie Oertle. In the background, Buddy Boy is ranting at Johnny. Frankie has now cradled himself in Georgia Tom's lap at the piano. Robert shifts his eyes and stares distantly beyond them, toward the bandstand.

GEORGIA TOM

"Woman, you readin' the *Ladies' Home Journal—*"

FRANKIE

"Yes, daddy—but I want that *Saturday Evenin'* Post!"

FAST DISSOLVE.

138. INTERIOR. RISING SUN CAFÉ. LATE NIGHT.

A driving rhythm rocks the stomping joint. On the bandstand, Robert leads Calvin and Johnny on guitar into "I Believe I'll Dust My Broom."

ROBERT (singing)

"I'm goin' get up in the mornin', I believe I'll dust my broom./ But when that black man you done lovin', girl, his friends can get my room—"

Robert's guitar produces an amazing mixture of barrelhouse piano and surging bass rhythms. Dead serious, his bald head glistening with sweat, he lowers his shoulder and rocks toward the dancers.

ROBERT (singing)

"I'm goin' write a letter, telephone every town I know./ If I can't find her in West Helena, she must be in East Monroe, I know—"

Frankie Jaxon dances intensely, joyfully, bumping and grinding through the wave of emotion on the floor.

Buddy Boy Hawkins has resumed his pleading with Oertle at the corner table. Brow furrowed, fisted knuckles tapping to the rhythm, an engrossed Oertle ignores him.

BUDDY BOY

Now you jus' listen here, Mr. Oertle, sir, you jus' listen on up here to Buddy Boy Hawkins one more time—

FRANKIE (off)

Oh, HONEY! Oh, KISS me now! Right THERE!

FAST DISSOLVE.

139. INTERIOR. RISING SUN CAFÉ. MIDNIGHT.

An exciting epiphany of song and dance. "Dust My Broom" is thundering now with Georgia Tom on piano, Frankie Jaxon hooting and strutting all over, Robert Johnson, head shaved, singing and wringing his guitar, with a cluster of six seated guitarists, knees interlocked and guitars kissing, creating a remarkable wall of rhythm from behind.

Singing, rocking, playing guitar with all his might, Robert is in control out front on the bandstand.

ROBERT (singing)

"I'm goin' call up Chiney, see is my good girl over there./ If I can't find her on Philippines Island, she must be in Ethiopia somewhere—"

Sloppily drunk Buddy Boy is still begging Oertle in the chaos, his voice scarcely audible.

BUDDY BOY

I goin' do it, sir, you see, this "Awful Fix" o' mine is the worst, is the saddest song in history, I goin' do it, sir—

OERTLE

Oh, Buddy Boy, you did that nine years ago. You know it didn't sell.

BUDDY BOY

I goin' do it again, sir. Better'n this young sucker there, sir—

Robert lunges and pivots on the wooden platform. A feverish peak.

FRANKIE

Oh, if I die, let me die while I'm HAPPY! I'm dyin' for You, Lord! Hot DAMN!

140. INTERIOR. RISING SUN CAFÉ. AFTER MIDNIGHT.

The joint is more subdued now. Robert, drinking at the bar, is crowded by admirers and backslappers. He is restless, oblivious to it all.

On the bandstand, forty-year-old Buddy Boy Hawkins accompanies himself on guitar with his sad, moving "Awful Fix." His heartful voice reaches for the shadows.

BUDDY BOY (singing)

"Hey, mama, tell me what have I, what have I done,/ Because seem like you tryin' to ease your lovin' fair brown down—"

Oertle, sipping his beer pensively, is unaffected by the emotional performance. When he sees Robert leaving with Johnny and Calvin, Oertle follows.

BUDDY BOY (singing)

"You gonna wake up one these mornin's, sweet mama, I'll be gone/ An' you may not never see me in yo' town no mo'—"

Buddy Boy watches Oertle exit but continues singing.

141. EXTERIOR. RISING SUN CAFÉ. AFTER MIDNIGHT.

Oertle moves with Robert away from his friend and the milling bar crowd, crossing the desolate street. They pause to talk in the somber moonlight.

OERTLE

I got your name from Henry Speir down in Jackson. I'm Ernie Oertle, field representative, the American Record Company. Young man, I like your style—you're doin' somethin' strange and good. And your guitar's mighty good as well. Now tell me this: how many of those songs do you have, all told?

ROBERT

I suppose 'bout twenty, thirty maybe. But they
ain't nothin', they just air songs. As many as
there is, I got.

OERTLE

Long as you have two. Now come with me over
here a minute.

As Oertle leads Robert away from Johnny and Calvin,
we hear Buddy Boy's desperately poignant singing inside.

OERTLE

If you like, son, I can arrange for you to
make some records, sell those songs of yours
to the Vocalion Company. They have a studio
in Texas. I can buy you a train ticket that'll
get you clear to San Antonio, no problem.
What do you say?

ROBERT

Yes, sir, I want that.

Oertle takes the bills from his wallet and discreetly
shows them to Robert.

OERTLE

Okay, that's fifty bucks there. You can count—
there's an even fifty, certain. Now, Bob, you
gotta keep in mind this deal is serious, meaning
you're a professional from here on in, a recording artist for the American Record Company.
We're as tight as a horse's ass, everything on

schedule and in order. In the morning I'll meet you here with the money, then we'll grab a coupla beers somewhere and get you on that train. When you get to San Antonio, first you'll go find the Gunter Hotel, an' ask for a fella there named Don Law—

DISSOLVE.

142. INTERIOR. SHACK. WEE HOURS.

The party is over and the dimly lit shack is a mess. Tearful, grief-stricken Calletta wraps herself in an old gray shawl and exits. Dressed in their party suits, Joe and Esau look on.

143. EXTERIOR. COTTON FIELDS. WEE HOURS.

Calletta, wrapped in her shawl, hurries down a dirt path into the far gray fields.

DISSOLVE.

144. EXTERIOR. WEST HELENA STREET. WEE HOURS.

Bar patrons stroll and stagger silently up the street. Oertle is seen shaking off persistent Buddy Boy.

OERTLE (hushed)

No, Buddy Boy, sorry, Walter, no—

BERRY VENDOR

Black-berry black, ge' blackberry black black ber-ry, black ber-ry—

The old vendor wanders along, chanting gently.

145. EXTERIOR. BATHHOUSE. WEE HOURS.

Robert, Johnny and Calvin approach a sign over a store-front reading "West Helena/ BATHS/ colored."

CALVIN

Hacksaw, he said they had his head in a horn o' some kind, an' he have to pull his head out for the words, then put it back in to sing. But he said they keep you good an' drunk, all likkered up, for free—

They pause beneath the sign.

JOHNNY

This is it, man. Room's upstairs. Guess I'll get on back to my cows.

Robert hands Johnny some money, exits. He pockets it.

JOHNNY

You don't owe me nothin', man.

CALVIN

We catch you 'fore too long—

DISSOLVE.

146. EXTERIOR. LEVEE. WEE HOURS.

Calletta hurries along atop the distant levee. Finally she stops. Weeping, she holds herself sorrowfully.

DISSOLVE.

147. INTERIOR. BATHHOUSE. WEE HOURS.

A dark, impersonal room. Robert is staring at his image

in the mirror. He removes his shirt, drapes it over his upright guitar and slips into bed.

The sad low chant of the blackberry vendor drifts up from the street. An eerie, faraway calling.

VENDOR (off)

Black-berry black; looka blackberry dozen an' blackberry fine; ease yo' black-blood, ol' friend o' mine—

Facing the open window, lying in bed on his side, Robert stares blankly, biting his lip. He rolls over and faces the darkness.

VENDOR (off)

Yessuh, how much—

SLOW DISSOLVE.

148. EXTERIOR. SAN ANTONIO TRAIN DEPOT. DAWN.

A cold mist at daybreak. Standing on the corner of the terminal building, alone, a tall stout black man wearing three gray overcoats and no shoes. He is playing his guitar and singing with utter joy, his big voice ringing.

RAGTIME (singing)

"Heyyyy, Jonah, halll-lelujah! Heyyyy, Jonah, preachin' in that wilderness—"

The charismatic hobo smiles broadly while playing to the camera. He strums his old guitar vigorously.

RAGTIME

"Go down yonder to the bottom of the ship,/
See you can find the dirty blue-eyed Christian/

Soon to come after, so say the Lord./ Could not
find the blue-eyed Christian—"

With primitive bamboo panpipes hanging from his neck,
solitary Ragtime stomps his bare foot, singing merrily.
His breath is visible in the chilly gray air.

RAGTIME (singing)

"Had Brother Jonah sent overboard,/ Cast the
bird an' dropped the seed,/ Dropped the seed
'long came the root,/ From the root is that
strong vine—"

A POLICEMAN enters with billy club. A train whistle
blows.

RAGTIME (singing)

"From the vine is that strong shade,/ Under
that shade Brother Jonah laid—"

POLICEMAN

Le's move along now, Ragtime.

Smiling at the passing officer, Ragtime does not miss a
beat. A closer look clearly suggests his guitar is string-
less. Playing, singing joyfully, he turns and wanders off.

RAGTIME (singing)

"When I get to hea-ven, I will sit an' tell,/ I escaped both death an' hell./ Heyyy, Jonah, hal-
lelujah!—"

A Texas & Pacific freight and passenger train pulls in.

SUPER: "San Antonio, Texas, November 1936"

143

149. EXTERIOR. TRAIN DEPOT PLATFORM. SUNRISE.

An old TRAIN CALLER chants as passengers embark and disembark. Sheep are unloaded from a freight car beyond.

CALLER

All out for the Sun-shine Special! Change cars on the T.P.! Fort Worth! Dallas! Silver Lake! Mineola! Garden City! El Dorado! Tex-ark-ana!—

Weary Robert traverses the platform with his guitar on his back. Wearing a dark suit and white shirt, his hair has grown back in a bit.

CALLER (off)

Change from the Katy! Pine Bluff! Magnolia! Hopeville! Territory!

TAMALE VENDOR

Red-hot tamales! An' they're red-hot tamales! Oh, tamales, oh! Oh, tamales, ah! Red-hot tamales!

Robert buys a tamale and weaves his way out to the street.

FAST DISSOLVE.

150. EXTERIOR. HAT SHOP. MORNING.

Fixing the brim on his new brown hat, Robert leaves the store and moves into the brilliant sunlight.

151. EXTERIOR. LUKENBACH BAR. LATE MORNING.

He follows two attractive black women into the bar. The noise from within is audible outside.

152.   INTERIOR. LUKENBACH BAR. LATE MORNING.

Robert leans on the bar, drinking a pint of whiskey. He eyes the attractive women drinking nearby. A jukebox plays a popular Mexican corrido, shouting above the din.

Guzzling his booze, Robert watches the women move toward an empty table. At the adjacent table, two black men and one white, all wearing cowboy hats, carry on loudly.

> BLACK COWBOY 1

Wo sterben die meisten Leute?

> WHITE COWBOY

Im Bett natürlich.

> BLACK COWBOY 2

Sie haben aber keine Furcht, jeden Abend ins Bett zu steigen!

> WHITE COWBOY

HO-pa! Landsleute!

Robert approaches the women. They look him over.

> ROBERT

Excuse me, uh, ladies, can you tell this stranger where's the Gunter Hotel?

The first black cowboy stands, glaring at Robert. The tall muscleman walks over, yanks one of the women to her feet and kisses her passionately. The crowded bar erupts with cheers. Robert swipes money off his table, exits.

FAST DISSOLVE.

153. EXTERIOR. SAN ANTONIO STREET. AFTERNOON.

Robert wanders along eating another tamale. He tosses
it into a bin and moves on. A tramp eagerly fishes for
the refuse, tasting the wrapper.

154. EXTERIOR. GUNTER HOTEL. LATE AFTERNOON.

Standing outside the "Looking Back Bar," Robert beholds the hotel's impressive facade across the street. A
deafening police siren scares him. Robert turns and
enters the noisy bar as a big Greyhound bus passes by.

155. INTERIOR. "LOOKING BACK BAR." LATE AFTERNOON.

General clamor in another commotive joint. A blues
harp is wailing deliriously. Robert enters and pushes his
way through the milling black patrons toward the bar.

Kneeling on the wet floor, the harp player blows
furiously, louder and louder. The crowd presses in, urg-
ing him on, fists clenched. An emotional little black man
kneels beside the possessed harp player. Overcome, he
breaks down heavily into tears.

Robert is at the bar finishing another pint of whiskey.
He surveys the reeling room, then signals for a second
round. He is approached by a corpulent, eager wench,
fortyish.

WILLIE MAE

I's a handsome woman. You's a handsome man.

ROBERT (to bartender)

Make that two, nigger.

WILLIE MAE

I's Willie Mae Cross.

ROBERT (looking away)

Bob Johnson.

The kneeling harp player, playing loud as can be, tries mightily for the impossible note. Kneeling next to him, the hysterical onlooker pleads for the harp player to stop.

WILLIE MAE (off)

You got money, lover?

DISSOLVE.

156. INTERIOR. GUNTER HOTEL LOBBY. TWILIGHT.

A modest lobby, with white clientele and hotel employees walking about. A dreamy half-light. Duke Ellington's vocalist Ivie Anderson sings sweetly on a radio.

RADIO

"Don't know why there's no sun up in the sky, stormy weather—"

Beneath cardboard letters spelling "Happy Thanksgiving" a lithe young blonde woman with her official hotel vest undone scans the somnambulistic lobby, her finger tapping a steamy radiator. Robert enters and looks about awkwardly. Lovely FAYE catches his eye briefly, rubbing her sexy ass against the warm beige coils.

RADIO

"Life is bad, gloom and misery everywhere, stormy weather./ Just can't get my poor self together—"

A BELLHOP in a snappy red outfit queries Robert. As he
does so, Faye steps up.

BELLHOP

The studio's on the seventh floor, but I'm afraid—

FAYE

Let me take care of him. Thisaway—

She leads him toward the open elevator, and the curly-
haired elevator operator C. J. DARWIN.

C.J.

Goin' up an', comin' down—

They enter with C.J., who closes the door.

157.   INTERIOR. HOTEL HALLWAY. TWILIGHT.

The door opens, and Robert follows Faye down the hallway to a door on the left. C.J. knocks, then they enter.

158.   INTERIOR. HOTEL ROOM. TWILIGHT.

A small, cluttered room. Faye leads Robert in. C.J. shuts
the door behind him. Faye is quietly undressing beside a
night table.

C.J.

Hold your peace, good boy.

Robert turns around. He sees Faye removing her skirt.
He addresses C.J.

ROBERT

I'm lookin' for Mr. Don Law.

C.J.

I'm Mrs. C. J. Darwin. An' this child here's my
baby sister Faye.

Naked Faye writhes seductively on the bed, her long
body smooth and serpentine. She glances at Robert,
then leans down on her forearms, eyes closed, purring.

C.J. (off)

We're gonna ask you to perform a coupla little
numbers for us, Mr. Recordin' Star—

C.J. closes her eyes, purses her lips, loosens a button.
Robert gently twists the knob and opens the door a slit.

159. INTERIOR. HOTEL HALLWAY. NIGHTFALL.

Robert carefully shuts the door and steals down the car-
peted hall, ducking into an "Exit" doorway while muttering, "Forgive me," under his breath.

A uniformed black hotel guard rounds the far corner
and walks expressionlessly toward the camera.

160. INTERIOR. RECORDING STUDIO. NIGHT.

A dark, empty chamber. A spray of light through an
open window, an armchair, a simple wooden chair near
a stand-up microphone. The studio is a converted hotel
room, with a makeshift observation window in a side
wall.

Robert enters. He steps to the microphone, then sits. He
holds the guitar across his lap but does not play it. A
stillness. Quietly, pining sweetly, he sings to himself.

ROBERT (singing)

"I got a kindhearted woman, do anythin' this

world for me./ I got a kindhearted mama, do anythin' this world for me—"

Robert leans forward, his lips near the dead microphone.

ROBERT (singing) (fast)

"But these evilhearted women, man, they will not let me—"

He looks over his right shoulder, singing. He rises and delicately leans his guitar against the chair.

ROBERT (singing)

"She's a kindhearted mama, studies evil all the time./ Got a kindhearted woman—"

Robert steps to the window. He runs his hand over the sill and examines the curtains.

ROBERT (singing)

"You wish to kill me, else to have it on your mind—"

The dim yellow lights switch on. Robert tenses up. The calm voice of an Englishman emerges.

DON LAW (off)

Easy, spider; I ain't gonna sweep—

Law is a tall, handsome, brown-haired man in his early thirties, wearing dark trousers, a white shirt with rolled sleeves and tie. Robert does not move as Law steps inside and faces him from the open door.

LAW

Easy now—what is it you're looking for?

ROBERT

Mr. Don Law. Gotta find him. The man in charge what's makin' the records. He's expectin' me.

LAW

I'm Mr. Law. Who are you?

ROBERT

Uh—Bob, Johnson. One of the talents, sir.

LAW

How'd you make it up here, Bob?

ROBERT

Give 'em my name, sir.

DISSOLVE.

161.   INTERIOR. RECORDING SUITE. LATE MORNING.

Two white recording assistants gaze through the observation window into the studio, at a polka band on break. Accordions, glockenspiels, a bass drum reading "ADOLPH and the BOHEMIANS." Law and Robert wander by.

LAW

Yes, Mr. Oertle told me about you; he mentioned a nice number you have for us, the one about a broom. You're a youngster, what, eighteen, nineteen?

ROBERT

Yessir, that's right, twenty-four, -five—

LAW

Where's your home?

ROBERT

The Delta. Yazoo Delta. Robinsonville. Mississippi, in around there. Arkansas some—West Helena. Like that.

Inside the studio we can see the polka band gulping down bottles of whiskey and steins of beer.

LAW (off)

Any family to speak of?

ROBERT (off)

Few brothers, sisters scattered about. Imagine my mother's down in Commerce. Never knowed my father. Name was Noah. Hard to say.

162. INTERIOR. REHEARSAL ROOM. NOON.

Another converted hotel room, with cowboy and Mexican musicians milling about, eating sandwiches. Robert sits head down on a corner chair, picking his guitar, mumbling. Law stands over him, his hand resting on a microphone. A bottle of whiskey is on the floor between them.

LAW

Now, Bob, we run things pretty much on time around here. You don't just likker up an' play— we want to know what you play, how you play it, meaning words to the songs and all, and how long you take to do a song. No song may exceed three minutes. Do you practice much?

ROBERT (mumbling)

—mistreated, reason why . . . yessir, all the time, myself, no one else—

Robert grabs the bottle and drinks up, briefly glancing at Law, who speaks. Robert's eyes drop again.

LAW

Like I said, we provide you with all the drink you'll need. And when you have to go: downstairs, hotel policy. Now, have you ever been behind a microphone before?

ROBERT (mumbling)

—wring my hands . . . no, sir, uh-uh.

LAW

Well, we use a Western Electric condenser mike. It's not so hot and humid these days but, if anything goes wrong, we can switch to a carbon mike setup. The main thing for you to remember about this microphone, Bob, is this: you must never forget it is there.

ROBERT (mumbling)

—slow the dark, slow the dark come down . . . never forget, no, sir—

163. INTERIOR. RECORDING STUDIO. AFTERNOON.

From across the sunlit room we see Law pointing to two

light bulbs on the wall. Robert sits facing the microphone in the corner, guitar ready, bottle at his feet.

LAW

Look here, Bob. Look here for one second.

Robert mumbles "Yessir" and glances up momentarily.

LAW

These two lights are important. Now, this is the
blue one: when you are recording, this blue
light stays on for three minutes. When three
minutes of singing time are up—now I am looking at the red one—this red light flashes on. It
might be a good idea to practice staring at
them—

Law stares at Robert, who stares at the microphone. As
Law steps toward the door, Robert sends a deep twang
echoing softly across the chamber.

164. INTERIOR. RECORDING BOOTH. AFTERNOON.

Reaching the doorway, Law calls back to Robert.

LAW

Tell me, Bob—do you want a microphone down
by your feet?

No response. One of Law's assistants speaks up.

JIMMY

Maybe he needs a pillow.

Seeing a Mexican group in the rehearsal room, Law
sends Jimmy to get them. As he does so, Law addresses
Robert via loudspeaker.

LAW

Say, you look pretty jittery out there.

ROBERT (via speaker)

—love my baby, can't make that agree . . . yessir, this shakin's what keeps me steady, sir—

The Mexican sextet enters with guitars and sombreros.

165. INTERIOR. RECORDING STUDIO. AFTERNOON.

Three smiling women and three smiling men come in.
Robert sits with his back to them in the corner. Law
speaks through the tinny loudspeaker overhead, standing behind the window.

LAW (via speaker)

Bob . . . Bob, before you start in, the Barraza
sisters wanted to loosen you up a bit, make you
feel more at home—

Robert turns around to see the vivacious musicians burst
into song, the women singing lead.

BARRAZAS (singing)

"*Voy a cantarle, señor, todo lo que
sufrí./ Desde que deje mi patria por venir a
este país—*"

As Robert stands facing them, tentatively, politely, leaning back as they close in, the Mexicans give him the biggest smiles he has ever seen.

BARRAZAS (singing)

"*Adiós, mi madre querida, hechame su bene-
dición./ Yo me voy al extranjero, donde no
hay revolución—*"

LAW (via speaker)

These folks have quite a few hits with us, Bob.
Mr. Berlanga in the middle there and his partner Mr. Montalvo have had I don't know how
many, which ones, let me see—

Beyond the glass, Law fumbles through ledger sheets as,
surrounding Robert, the jubilant singers continue. Robert is terrified. He sits, turns and faces the corner.

BARRAZAS (singing)

*"Cruce por fin la frontera, y en un renganche
salí./ Ay, mi querido extranjero, fué mucho lo
que sufrí—"*

They close in on Robert, and the camera. Law looks on.
Robert yearns for silence. He looks up at the blinking
red light.

166. INTERIOR. RECORDING STUDIO. LATE AFTERNOON.

The red light is blinking over Robert, sitting alone. He
picks the guitar nervously, mumbling to himself, waiting. He swigs his whiskey bottle. Behind the pane of
glass, Law stands with his two assistants by the recording machine ready to begin.

LAW (via speaker)

Master number 25-84, take 1, Robert Johnson,
stand by—

Robert glances at the blinking red light. Holding a clipboard, Law waits.

ROBERT (mumbling)

—wonder could I sympathize, 'pologize; or
would she sympathize, to me—

156

LAW (via speaker)

Ready now, rolling—

The blue light glows steadily as Robert leans toward the microphone, playing the first startling guitar chords before descending into a chugging bass rhythm. His voice is passionate, filled with an innocent pleading.

ROBERT (singing)

"When you got a good friend, that will stay right by your side/ Give her all your spare time, love an' treat her right—"

CLOSEUP of Robert from inside his corner. His lips are inches from the microphone.

ROBERT (singing)

"I mistreated my baby, an' I can't see no reason why./ Every time I think about it, I jus' wring my hands an' cry—"

Law watches Robert fixedly as his assistants stare at the machines. The rhythm of the song gradually quickens. Robert sings with his eyes momentarily closed, his teeth clenched.

ROBERT (singing)

"It's your opinion, friendgirl, that I may be right or wrong/ But when you watch your close friends, baby, your enemies can't do you no harm—"

FAST DISSOLVE.

167. INTERIOR. RECORDING BOOTH. LATE AFTERNOON.

Through the observation window we see blades of sunlight cutting through the darkening studio. The red light blinks on the wall. Robert polishes off another bottle in his dim corner, a streak of light behind his back, climbing the wall. Law's aide ART replaces the spent bottle.

Law enters the booth. Jimmy exits momentarily. Art returns. Law speaks into his microphone.

LAW

Master number 26-29, take 2, Robert Johnson, stand by—

The studio light is switched on, casting a jaundiced pall over the room. A car horn honks faintly outside. Jimmy returns. We see Robert drinking from his bottle.

168. INTERIOR. RECORDING STUDIO. LATE AFTERNOON.

Robert wipes his lip and waits tensely. The blinking red bulb goes dark, the blue light glows. Robert attacks his next song with nine jangling strums, a jarring prelude.

ROBERT (singing)

"I went to the crossroad, fell down on my knee,/ Asked the Lord above, 'Have mercy, save poor Bob if You please—'"

Behind the glass, Law writes something down and hands the clipboard to Art. Robert performs the monumental song with controlled fury, sliding and plucking his big guitar.

ROBERT (singing)

"Mmmm sun goin' down, ooooo! dark gonna catch me here./ Haven't got no lovin' sweet woman to love an' feel my care—"

Reaching for emotional peaks, Robert sometimes throws his head away from the microphone. Over his shoulder we see a displeased Law in the booth, shaking his head.

169. INTERIOR. RECORDING STUDIO. TWILIGHT.

The red light is blinking over Robert's head as he mops his brow, then gulps down some whiskey. Art is opening up the curtains behind him. Law speaks from the booth while the song is played back.

LAW (via speaker)

Bob, Bob, the microphone. You're doing good work, but you mustn't forget that mike there—

PLAYBACK

"You can run, you can run, tell my friendboy Willie Brown,/ Lord, that I'm standin' at the crossroad, baby, I believe I'm sinkin' down—"

In the booth, Jimmy knots his tie and dons his jacket. Robert faces the corner, holding his bottle, listening.

FAST DISSOLVE.

170. INTERIOR. RECORDING BOOTH. MORNING.

CLOSEUP of the recording machines playing back the end to the ominous "Come On in My Kitchen."

PLAYBACK

"Wintertime comin', it's gonna be slow./ You can't make the winter, babe, this dry long soul—"

Jimmy and Art prepare the machines. Law steps to his mike.

171. INTERIOR. RECORDING STUDIO. MORNING.

As if he has not moved since yesterday, from across the floor we see Robert seated, facing the corner, the bottle of whiskey by his foot. The room is awash with sunlight.

LAW (via speaker)

Master number 25-86, take 1, Robert Johnson, stand by—

The red light gives way to the blue. Robert unleashes his relentlessly exciting "Terraplane Blues."

ROBERT (singing)

"An' I feel so lonesome, you hear me when I moan./ Who been drivin' my Terraplane for you since I been gone?—"

In Robert's performing frenzy, he seems to be playing several guitar parts at once. A dazzling, brilliant display.

ROBERT (singing)

"I flashed my lights, mama, this horn won't even blow./ Got a short in this connection hoo-wherever, way down below—"

172. INTERIOR. RECORDING BOOTH. MORNING.

Law and his assistants gaze through their reflections on the glass at Robert, whose singing is at a peak now.

ROBERT (via speaker)

"Mr. Highwayman, plea-hease! don't block the road/ 'Cause she registrin' a cold one hundred./ I'm booked an' I got to go—"

160

ART

Kid sounds good—

LAW (muttering)

That damn head of his—

ROBERT (via speaker)

"Eeeee-HEEEEEEE! You hear me weep an' moan—"

FAST DISSOLVE.

173. INTERIOR. RECORDING STUDIO. AFTERNOON.

The blinking red light goes off, the blue turns on and Robert introduces a bouncing, playful new rhythm.

ROBERT (singing)

"If I send for my baby, man, an' she don't come/ All the doctors in Hot Springs sure can't help her none—"

Robert unexpectedly flashes a glance behind him toward Don Law, then turns back to the microphone.

ROBERT (singing)

"An' if she gets unruly, thinks she don't wanna do,/ Take my .32-20 now an' cut her half in two—"

Big ADOLPH HOFNER swigs his beer in the booth, looking on with the others approvingly, nodding with the beat.

ROBERT (singing)

"Gonna shoot my pistol, gonna shoot my Gatlin' gun./ You made me love you, now your man have come—"

174. INTERIOR. RECORDING BOOTH. AFTERNOON.

CLOSEUP of the heavy steel recording needle cutting into the spinning black master.

ROBERT (via speaker)

"Her .38 Special, boys, it do very well./ I got a .32-20 now, an' it's a-burnin' . . ."

FAST DISSOLVE.

175. INTERIOR. RECORDING STUDIO. LATE AFTERNOON.

With the golden blades of sunlight streaking about the room, Robert sings in a strange, guttural voice, playing his quickest, most insistent, dizzying rhythm.

ROBERT (singing)

"I got a girl say she long an' tall, sleeps in the kitchen with her feets in the hall./ Hot tamales an' they're red hot, yeah, she got 'em for sale!"

FAST DISSOLVE.

176. INTERIOR. RECORDING BOOTH. LATE AFTERNOON.

Law, rubbing his chin, listens to a playback. Robert is drinking in his corner inside, the red bulb blinking.

PLAYBACK

"I got dead shrimps, babe, someone's fishin' in my pond—"

CLOSEUP of Law, his brow furrowed, concentrating hard.

FAST DISSOLVE.

177. INTERIOR. RECORDING STUDIO. TWILIGHT.

Robert puts the bottle down as Law speaks into his microphone. The dim electric light smothers the tired room.

LAW (via speaker)

Master number 26-31, take 1, Robert Johnson, stand by—

The yellowish studio lights quiver. The blue bulb glows. Robert initiates a lively, easy rhythm.

ROBERT (singing)

"It's the last fair deal gone down,/ Last fair deal gone down, good Lord, on the Gulfport Island Road—"

Law steps out of the booth, momentarily vacant now.

ROBERT (singing)

"Ida Bell, don't cry this time,/ If you cry 'bout a nickel, you'll die 'bout a dime./ You cry, but the money, it ain't mine—"

The driving rhythm gains momentum.

178. INTERIOR. REHEARSAL ROOM. TWILIGHT.

An assortment of German, Mexican and Texas cowboy musicians drinking, practicing, chatting, milling about. Law is in the background, closing the curtains on the windows. Robert's voice rings in over the tinny loudspeaker.

ROBERT (via speaker)

"I like the way you do,/ I love the way you do, good Lord, on this Gulfport Island Road—"

A sudden explosive acceleration of rhythm in the song. Law turns and makes an announcement.

LAW

That is all for today, my friends. After this one we'll be closing early. I want each of you to have a pleasant evening. Until tomorrow.

The musicians start packing, leaving, finishing drinks.

179. INTERIOR. RECORDING STUDIO. TWILIGHT.

In the far dark corner, Robert sits alone, his up-tempo performance churning.

ROBERT (singing)

"My Captain's so mean on me,/ My Captain's so mean, ohhh! good Lord—"

180. INTERIOR. RECORDING BOOTH. TWILIGHT.

As the song ensues Law steps back inside the booth, looks through the window at Robert, picks up his clipboard.

ROBERT (via speaker)

"I'm workin' my way back home,/ I'm workin' my way back home, good Lord—"

Jimmy and Art re-enter the booth and check the machines.

181. INTERIOR. RECORDING STUDIO. TWILIGHT.

From across the room we watch Robert singing in his corner, the window on the wall beside him turning deep blue, with Law partially visible through the observation window.

Robert somehow conjures church bells out of his guitar as he maintains the melody and bass lines simultaneously. He repeats it seconds later.

182.   INTERIOR. RECORDING BOOTH. NIGHTFALL.

The red light is blinking over Robert's bowed head inside as Law and his assistants prepare for closing.

> JIMMY
>
> I have a hunch he'll sell like hell.

> ART
>
> Impressive. No doubt about it.

> LAW (into microphone)
>
> I think we'll call it a day, Bob. On your way out stop here and Jimmy will give you—no, Art will give you your forty-five cents for the room. (Aside, to Art: I hope he'll hold onto it.)

> JIMMY
>
> Don't worry, we'll make it back.

Robert polishes off the last bottle. The red light blinks.

183.   INTERIOR. GUNTER HOTEL LOBBY. NIGHT.

Robert walks wearily out of the elevator and straight for the door. C.J. watches him, then casts a glance over to the desk clerk, who signals Faye.

184.   EXTERIOR. GUNTER HOTEL. NIGHT.

Robert exits the hotel, slings his guitar onto his back and fixes his hat. Over his shoulder, Faye and C.J. stand at a window pointing Robert out to a uniformed white COP.

Across the street, Willie Mae stands on the curb outside the bar. She sees Robert walk down the steps and along the sidewalk. As a big Greyhound bus rumbles between them, she starts following him.

The cop steps outside, his eye trained on Robert.

185. EXTERIOR. SAN ANTONIO STREET. NIGHT.

Trudging down an empty side street, Robert glances back and notices the quick-stepping cop, who immediately slows down and looks innocently about him. Robert continues on at a faster pace. Willie Mae, losing ground, still trails him.

186. EXTERIOR. SAN ANTONIO DRUGSTORE. NIGHT.

Robert hurries past Ayala's Drugstore where a crowd is blocking our view of a young black singer-guitarist.

> SINGER
>
> "Gonna get up in the mornin', do like Buddy Brown./ I'm gonna eat my breakfast, rider, an' lay back down—"

The cop rushes to the front of the crowd, looks the young singer over suspiciously, moves on.

187. EXTERIOR. PRODUCE MARKET. NIGHT.

Robert races through the outdoor market as the stands shut down. Several Mexican, black and cowboy street singers are setting up at scattered points. The cop is given directions by an ELDERLY BLACK MAN across the street.

ELDERLY BLACK MAN

Yessir, young man run to the Manure Plaza there, sure as I'm alive—

Blowing his whistle now, the cop runs into the dark marketplace, past a Mexican singer and an aproned vendor. He glimpses Robert running fifty yards ahead, snaking between vegetable carts, vendors, singers, listeners, before falling down, knocking a drunken black man down as well.

The cop hustles forward for the kill. Bearing his club, he leaps upon the fallen man and starts pummeling him. An excited crowd gathers for the black-white slugfest.

When a produce truck labeled "Moon" passes nearby, we see Robert look back momentarily from across the street, then he hurries on as the cop keeps beating the drunken man.

188. EXTERIOR. ALLEY. NIGHT.

Robert mops his brow while wandering up the dark, dank alley. Wandering toward him is a pallid white woman, a WAIF in tattered clothes. They slow to a near standstill while passing. Her round face has ruby cheeks and big, bloodshot eyes. They exchange familiar stares. They stop moving. She comes on to him, whistling. She caresses his guitar.

WAIF

Mmm. I sing real good, lover—

WILLIE MAE (off)

You better tell your man from mine, chile—

Up the alley, Willie Mae stands with hands on hips, eyes

glaring. Robert takes note. Staring hard at the waif, he wanders backward tentatively.

WAIF (hushed)

Another time, man.

A sad grin on her forsaken face. She exits, hoarsely crowing "Down on Me" down the alley, distantly.

FAST DISSOLVE.

189. INTERIOR. GUNTER HOTEL DINING ROOM. NIGHT.

Eating their Thanksgiving dinner, Don Law, Art, Jimmy and Adolph sit in earnest conversation. His mouth stuffed as he wields a drumstick, Jimmy pontificates thoughtfully. A handsome black waiter pours the ice water.

JIMMY

Now, our country's a lot like this turkey here, my dad used to say. Because, see, it's got both the white-colored meat an' the dark-colored meat, with nerves runnin' through them all the same. More white maybe, but—

ART

Just remember, bein' born a nigger's the worst thing in this world, fella—

ADOLPH (toasting)

Gentlemen, gentlemen: humility! Let us not ignore America—

The three men lift their glasses as Law turns to the waiter.

168

LAW

LAW

More cranberry sauce, my boy—

FAST DISSOLVE.

190.   EXTERIOR. BOARDINGHOUSE. NIGHT.

An old frame house, with a sign reading "Board-inghouse/ transients—colored/ Mrs. E. Lincoln, Prop." An open window on the second floor.

191.   INTERIOR. BOARDINGHOUSE. NIGHT.

Lying in bed in the blue moonlight, Robert rests his tired head on fleshy Willie Mae's naked breast. She pats his brow tenderly, maternally. Faintly, a train whistle blows.

Robert's guitar is leaning against the wall. His shirt is draped over it from the neck.

WILLIE MAE

Bobby, I do believe I found me the man of my dreams. The man of my dreams—

There are tears in her tiny painted eyes. A car horn honks outside.

FAST DISSOLVE.

192.   EXTERIOR. TRAIN STATION PLATFORM. WEE HOURS.

Stillness. Ragtime sleeps soundly on a bench, a dormant passenger train behind. We hear footsteps.

Robert walks across the desolate platform holding a small suitcase, the guitar on his back. He boards the car designated "Colored." Sitting down inside, Robert's face shows in the row of blackened windows. He gazes blankly outside. Utter silence. A brakeman appears, swinging a lantern.

SLOW DISSOLVE.

193. EXTERIOR. CITY STREET. AFTERNOON.

In harsh summer sunlight, a sweet black FLOWER GIRL sings her innocent, melodic chant on the busy sidewalk.

FLOWER GIRL

Yes, ma'am, I got flowers. You ask me how I sell 'em:/ Ten cents, three for a quarter./ Now who got the money come an' buy, an' who ain't got the money kindly stand aside an' cry./ Flowers are goin' by—

SUPER: "Dallas, Texas, June 1937"

Turning a corner, a Greyhound bus comes briefly into view. A young gentleman buys his female companion a flower.

194. INTERIOR. RECORDING SUITE. AFTERNOON.

Don Law stands in the hallway, studying the ledger sheets on his clipboard. Through the nearby observation window we see the hazy studio's walls covered with long dark drapery. Two upright fans blow air over two white bathtubs filled with water and ice. A sweaty cowboy quintet is packing it in; three of them button their shirts as a fourth puts on his pants. Art enters and strolls toward the recording booth with Law. A fiddler passes by.

ART

Who's down next?

LAW

We'll let that Robert Johnson do one now, then
we'll finish him after the Light Crust Doughboys later—

195. INTERIOR. REHEARSAL ROOM. AFTERNOON.

Robert sits in the unlit, cluttered room wearing a dark
suit with dark hat, hunched over his big blond guitar.
He is studying his little black book, sweating heavily.

ART (off)

So Johnson's the last one.

LAW (off)

I imagine that's enough for one Sunday. It's
been hot as blazes here.

ART (fading) (off)

Big week comin' up, once we're over this—

Staring at his open book, Robert removes his hat and
sets it on the floor. His hair seems long now, straight and
neatly combed. He raises his bottle slowly.

LAW (via speaker)

Robert Johnson. Studio. Waiting for you.

Tilting his head back, Robert takes an enormous swig
from his whiskey bottle. Jimmy looks on from the doorway.

196. INTERIOR. RECORDING STUDIO. LATE AFTERNOON.

From across the floor we see Robert facing the corner,
surrounded by long dark curtains, a red light blinking
on the wall overhead. Law stands at his microphone.

LAW (via speaker)

Master number 3-77, take 1, Robert Johnson, stand by—

From inside his corner we see Robert clearly now. With
his long straight hair, wearing a black shirt under his
dark suit, his appearance is much stranger than before.
Art enters the booth beyond, looking in beside Law. The
blue light flashes on.

ROBERT (singing)

"I got stones in my passway, an' my road seem
dark as night./ I have pains in my heart, they
have taken my appetite—"

Robert's voice is humble, resigned, his guitar playing
subtle and dramatic. He is sweating noticeably.

ROBERT (singing)

"I have a bird to whistle, an' I have a bird to
sing./ I got a woman that I'm lovin', boy, but
she don't mean a thing—"

197. INTERIOR. RECORDING BOOTH. LATE AFTERNOON.

Law leaves the booth for a moment. Art follows.

ROBERT (via speaker)

"My enemies have betrayed me, have overtaken
poor Bob at last—"

CLOSEUP of the needle cutting the spinning black master.
A sudden shift in the song's rhythm.

ROBERT (via speaker)

"Now you trying to take my life, an' all my

lovin' too./ You laid a passway for me, now what are you tryin' to do—"

198.   INTERIOR. RECORDING STUDIO. LATE AFTERNOON.

Law and his assistants re-enter the booth as Robert hits the song's emotional peak. The blades of sunlight shift.

ROBERT (singing)

"I'm cryin', Plea-hease, please! Let us be friends./ An' when you hear me howlin' in my passway, rider, please! open your door an' let me in—"

FAST DISSOLVE.

199.   INTERIOR. RECORDING BOOTH. TWILIGHT.

Law listens carefully to the song in playback. Through the observation window we see Robert facing the corner, head down, the red light blinking on the wall.

PLAYBACK

"I got three legs to truck on, boys, please don't block my road—"

200.   INTERIOR. RECORDING STUDIO. TWILIGHT.

Robert remains head bowed, listening to the playback end.

PLAYBACK

"I been feelin' 'shamed 'bout my rider,/ Babe, I'm booked an' I got to go—"

Reaching for his bottle, Robert stares across the room at a middle-aged, skinny black janitor wringing his mop into a bucket. The janitor stares back. Then he picks up his bucket and slowly walks toward the door.

Jimmy enters and tries moving one of the water-laden bathtubs. Unable to, he exits. Law stands at his microphone as Robert glances up at the blinking red bulb. The door shuts tightly. A silence.

> LAW (via speaker)

Master number 3-77, take 2, Robert Johnson, stand by—

> ROBERT

I want to go on with the next one, myself.

> LAW (via speaker)

Master number 4-0-2, take 1, Robert Johnson, stand by—
> (pause)
It's rolling, Bob—

The red bulb darkens, the blue glows steadily. Robert plays the first shimmering, delicately descending chords to "Love in Vain." His voice is tender, helplessly sad.

> ROBERT (singing)

"I followed her to the station, with a suitcase in my hand./ Well, it's hard to tell it's hard to tell, when all your love's in vain./ All my love's in vain—"

From inside the corner we see Robert leaning in close to the microphone, with Law behind the glass observing alone. The steady beat takes hold. Jimmy enters the booth. With the studio lights still turned off, the natural half-light intensifies the atmosphere.

ROBERT (singing)

"When the train rolled up to the station, I looked her in the eye./ Well I was lonesome I felt so lonesome, an' I could not help but cry./ All my love's in vain—"

Law turns his head and gazes out of the booth.

201.   INTERIOR. RECORDING BOOTH. TWILIGHT.

Law is gazing at the camera, as through the window we see Robert facing the far corner, the blue light glowing, while the graceful blues ballad continues. Its melody and rhythm begin to converge, a forlorn tension builds.

ROBERT (via speaker)

"When the train, it left the station, with two lights on behind./ Well, the blue light was my blues, an' the red light was my mind./ All my love's in vain—"

Peering hard into the studio, Law dons a pair of bulky old headphones, pressing them to his ears tightly with both hands. The gentle force of the song suddenly swells.

202.   INTERIOR. REHEARSAL ROOM. TWILIGHT.

In the unlit, small cluttered room, the hanging loud-speaker carries forth Robert's desperate plaint. Beside his vacant chair lie his hat and empty whiskey bottle.

ROBERT (via speaker)

"Eeee hooooooooooo-ooooo! Willie Mae/ Oh oh oh hey heyy-ooooo! Willie Mae—"

203. INTERIOR. RECORDING STUDIO. TWILIGHT.

From inside his corner Robert closes his eyes, wringing his heart at the microphone. Law stands behind the glass with Jimmy, hands pressing his headphones.

ROBERT (via speaker)

"You-hoo-oooo, HEE-vee oh woe,/ All my love's, in vain—"

The red light blinks on.

204. INTERIOR. RECORDING STUDIO. NIGHT.

Across the floor, Robert swigs his whiskey bottle as the dull studio light is switched on. The red light continues to blink. Robert puts the bottle down. An ominous air.

Art enters and closes the heavy curtains over the darkening window. He tries moving one of the bathtubs as Law looks on. Art drags a fan away instead and exits.

LAW (via speaker)

Master number 3-9-8, take 1, Robert Johnson, stand by—

The blue light commences to glow over Robert's head. He introduces the song with a suspenseful, lunging rhythm on guitar. Law puts his headphones on. Art enters the booth.

ROBERT (singing)

"Early this mornin', when you knocked upon my door/ An' I said, 'Hello, Satan, I believe it's time to go—'"

Robert's lips almost touch the microphone as he sings very clearly, matter-of-factly.

ROBERT (singing)

"Me an' the Devil was walkin' side by side./ I'm goin' to beat my woman, until I get satisfied—"

205. INTERIOR. RECORDING BOOTH. NIGHT.

Law removes his headphones as the song unfolds.

ROBERT (via speaker)

"She say she don't see why, that I will dog her 'round./ (spoken: Now, babe, you ain't doin' me right now—)/ Must be that ol' evil spirit, so deep down in the ground—"

206. INTERIOR. RECORDING STUDIO. NIGHT.

Robert seems to be confiding in the microphone now.

ROBERT (singing)

"You may bury my body down by the highway side/ So my ol' evil spirit can get a Greyhound bus, an' ride—"

Robert ends the powerful song and drops his head. The red light starts blinking above him.

FAST DISSOLVE.

207. INTERIOR. TEXAS BARRELHOUSE. NIGHT.

SILENT IMAGE: A wild joint filled with dancing black men and women, and a pulsating spray of red light. Robert performs spiritedly. A shapely woman dances for him, lifting up her skirt, pursing her lips.

FAST DISSOLVE.

208.   INTERIOR. MEXICAN CAFÉ. NIGHT.

SILENT IMAGE: Another wild place, filled with dancing Mexican men and women. Robert is backed by a guitarist wearing a sombrero. Off camera, we hear sounds emerging from the recording studio.

LAW (via speaker) (off)

Say, Bob, have you been down to Mexico yet? Bob?

FAST DISSOLVE.

209.   INTERIOR. TEXAS BAR. NIGHT.

SILENT IMAGE: Robert is backed by a white pianist and a black snare drummer in a whirling cowboy bar. Off camera, footsteps enter the studio, and the sound of dragging bathtubs. A drunken cowgirl grabs Robert's hand and rubs it over her sweating buttocks.

ROBERT (off) (mumbling)

Mmm, Mexico—

LAW (via speaker) (off)

What's that? Chicago?

ROBERT (off)

Yessir, Chicago—

FAST DISSOLVE.

210.   INTERIOR. RECORDING STUDIO. NIGHT.

Robert guzzles down some whiskey, then glances furtively over his left shoulder. Behind him, the bathtubs and fans are gone. The red light is blinking. Law speaks.

LAW (via speaker)

Master number 3-9-4, take 2, Robert Johnson, stand by—

The blue light begins to glow. Robert introduces his last song, "Hellhound on My Trail," an alarmingly beautiful testament to terror and one of the greatest American musical recordings ever made.

ROBERT (singing)

"I got to keep movin', I got to keep movin',/ Blues fallin' down like hail, blues fallin' down like hail./ An' the days keep on mindin' me, there's a hellhound on my trail, hellhound on my trail—"

Robert's voice is desperate. Like his guitar playing, he deliberately mixes discord with the tumbling melody. Art joins Law and Jimmy in the booth beyond.

ROBERT (singing)

"If today was Christmas Eve, an' tomorrow was Christmas Day/ (spoken: Aw, wouldn't we have a time, baby—)/ All I need's my lil sweet rider, jus' to pass the time away,/ Uh-huh, the time away—"

Law puts his headphones on as Robert's amazing performance proceeds. A staggering, downward cadence. Law studies his clipboard. Jimmy and Art stare outward expressionlessly.

211. INTERIOR. RECORDING BOOTH. NIGHT.

The heavy tone arm cuts into the spinning black master.

ROBERT (singing)

"You sprinkled hotfoot powder all around my
door, all around my door./ It keep me with
ramblin' in mind, ri-der, every ol' place I go,
every ol' place I go—"

Beyond the glass, Robert strains, picking the guitar delicately.

212. INTERIOR. RECORDING STUDIO. NIGHT.

Robert sings the final verse. In the background, Law
and his two assistants observe blankly from the booth.

ROBERT (singing)

"I can tell the wind is risin', the leaves tremblin'
on the tree, tremblin' on the tree./ All I need's
my lil sweet woman, to keep my company,
mmmmmmmmm, my company—"

After the last fading touches on guitar, Robert grips the
guitar neck tightly and hangs his head. Behind him,
Jimmy wanders into the studio, followed by Art, as Law
examines his ledger sheets in the booth. Looking lost,
the assistants loiter beyond the oblivious Robert, drinking alone in his corner, the red light blinking overhead.

DISSOLVE.

213. INTERIOR. WHOREHOUSE. NIGHT.

SILENT IMAGE: Surrounded by black whores and their
clients, Robert performs on guitar, paying no attention
to advances made upon him by a scantily clad beauty.
We hear footsteps off camera in the recording studio.

FAST DISSOLVE.

214.   EXTERIOR. HIGHWAY. NIGHT.

SILENT IMAGE: A Greyhound bus speeds out of the blackness over the two-lane asphalt artery.

LAW (via speaker) (off)

Well, that's it, both takes exactly the same—

ROBERT (mumbling) (off)

It's all what's left of me, sir.

JIMMY (off)

Johnson, I just wanna tell you that the last one about the hound was pretty darn interesting, both takes. And "Terraplane" that you did before's already sellin' like hell, *damn* good, let me tell ya, I predicted it—

FAST DISSOLVE.

215.   INTERIOR. LEVEE CAMP. NIGHT.

SILENT IMAGE: Beneath a fluttering canvas overhang, lit by flickering candles and kerosene lamps, Robert plays for a typically volatile mob of rough levee workers and their women from town. In the foreground, a muscular bare-chested tough holds a long blade at the throat of his female partner as they dance closely.

LAW (via speaker) (off)

I'm going to have Art here give you some money to help take care of things. One hundred dollars. That will also be your advance on royalties.

ROBERT (off)

Yessir, thank you, sir, I'll be needin' that awhile.

A vicious brawl suddenly erupts. The bare-chested worker is brutally stabbed in the heart.

216. EXTERIOR. LEVEE CAMP. NIGHT.

SILENT IMAGE: The violence spills outside the tent. Calvin Frazier rushes up from the riverside, is jumped by a man in the bushes, flattens the assailant with a single punch. A man with a gun shoots Calvin in the wrist as Johnny Shines strips the man of his weapon. Calvin picks the gun up and shoots the man in the neck. Robert hurries over.

ROBERT (off)

—Every man have his share of dignity in this life, sir. Thank you, sir—

LAW (via speaker) (off)

Well, Bob, you've earned it. You did just fine. Something about you—you'll get your dignity.

FAST DISSOLVE.

217. INTERIOR. HOUSE PARTY. NIGHT.

SILENT IMAGE: Robert, dressed to the teeth in his double-breasted suit, a white flower in his lapel, croons before an all-redneck crowd of dancers. Johnny backs him up with wounded Calvin, who conceals his inability to play.

FAST DISSOLVE.

218. INTERIOR. JOOK JOINT. NIGHT.

SILENT IMAGE: Robert, his appearance altered again with

hair slicked straight back, clothes white and suspenders black, has eager women hanging all over him as his sidemen back him up. Robert steps back and motions for Johnny to take the lead, while guzzling some whiskey. When Johnny glances back, Robert has vanished. A drunken woman grabs Johnny and dances with him. Johnny is not enjoying himself now. We hear footsteps on the studio floor.

ROBERT (off)

Y'know, it say in the Bible that man come some-where east of Eden under God all the same, through pain an' love an' good an' evil conse-quence like a ship upon the sea, to live an' let live—

LAW (off)

Where are you heading next, Bob—back home to the Delta?

FAST DISSOLVE.

219. INTERIOR. BOARDINGHOUSE ROOM. NIGHT.

SILENT IMAGE: Robert is making love to a young, over-weight black woman, who manhandles him passionately onto his back.

ROBERT (off)

—'Cause when you get to the final end you gonna stay anyway, you gonna linger if you like it or not, this life you don't remember. . . . Yes-sir, you might say that, sir.

FAST DISSOLVE.

220. INTERIOR. BOARDINGHOUSE ROOM. NIGHT.

SILENT IMAGE: Robert is rolling in bed with a skinny woman. The door opens, and Johnny is led inside by the manager, a woman the size of a midget.

LAW (off)

It will be good going home, won't it, Bob?
Gives a fella a full feeling inside—

FAST DISSOLVE.

221. EXTERIOR. ROADSIDE JOOK. NIGHT.

SILENT IMAGE: A sign reads "Bunk's Place," as black men and women chat and carouse and shoot craps outside.

FAST DISSOLVE.

222. EXTERIOR. URBAN JOOK. NIGHT.

SILENT IMAGE: An electric sign reads "Whitechild's," as well-dressed city blacks hang out in between automobiles.

FAST DISSOLVE.

223. EXTERIOR. NORTHERN ROADSIDE JOINT. NIGHT.

SILENT IMAGE: A flashing red sign reads "Charley Moleman's" in front of the snow-covered roadhouse.

ROBERT (off)

I ain't exactly doin' that, Mr. Law.

A police car cruises by slowly.

224. INTERIOR. CHARLEY MOLEMAN'S. NIGHT.

SILENT IMAGE: Another striking change for Robert.

Dressed like a contemporary gangster in hat, suit and tie, he now plays guitar with an electric pickup. Johnny plays second guitar, and Calvin, his wrist bandaged, plays drums. Bold black letters on the bass drum spell "ROBERT JOHNSON."

Panic suddenly overcomes the dancing joint as police pour in wielding clubs and guns. The women strip and run as a man shoots out the lights. The naked women flee into the snowy blackness, their bodies blending with the night.

LAW (off)

Well, Bob, we wish you all the luck in the world. If you will let us know where you'll be, those checks will reach you right away. Then, maybe, we'll record some more. You never can tell.

225. EXTERIOR. CHARLEY MOLEMAN'S. LATE NIGHT.

SILENT IMAGE: The police have set the joint ablaze and escape in their cars. Robert leaves Johnny and Calvin behind a tree, runs to the burning structure and braves the flames to gaze inside.

Through the window we see Robert's wired guitar leaning against a chair, in flames. Johnny's guitar is already destroyed. As the bass drum catches fire, the "Robert Johnson" logo perishes.

We hear footsteps in the studio, then the closing of a door.

226. EXTERIOR. ROAD NEAR MOLEMAN'S. LATE NIGHT.

SILENT IMAGE: Robert races onto a paved roadway with the roadhouse blazing behind him. Tears flowing down

monica, performing a spectacularly strange tap dance on
the pavement. Cars veer to the side of the road and
many of the joint patrons return. Coins are tossed for
the hysterical performer as the night's gaiety is renewed.

Surrounded by headlights and people, Robert wails and
dances wildly amidst a shower of silvery coins. The fire
rages in the background.

FAST DISSOLVE.

227. EXTERIOR. WOODLAND. LATE NIGHT.

FADE IN SOUND: Flipping a coin as he steps through tall
grass, Robert approaches a clearing of fallen trees. Farther on, a moonlit row of Mississippi virgin pines is
adorned by slender ropes descending gracefully from
each treetop.

FADE OUT.

FADE IN.

228. EXTERIOR. MUSIC SHOP. AFTERNOON.

A black youth with a battered guitar follows Robert,
who examines his beautiful new guitar while heading
for the door. The youth, named HONEYBOY, continues
outside when Robert turns back toward the proprietor,
who is counting a mountain of coins.

ROBERT

Ever heard of someone name of Noah Johnson? He's my father, and, it's been on my mind,
mainly—

SUPER: "Greenwood, Mississippi, August 1938"

We see the proprietor shake his head and shrug his shoulders, counting the coins. Ike Zinnerman trudges by talking to himself outside.

IKE (muttering)

I was Gabriel Turner for thirty-one years. I was *born* Gabriel, an' then they started to callin' me Ike. That's all right, but that ain't me. Ain't Gabriel Turner neither. Praise Jesus. What the hell is goin' on. Lord have mercy—

RALPH and his comely wife LOUISE bring their broken Victrola to the proprietor. Honeyboy grabs Robert in the doorway. Louise looks Robert over furtively.

HONEYBOY

—an' I'd sincerely like to back you some, Mr. Johnson. I know all your records like "Terraplane" an' (sings) "I got a kindhearted woman—"

With the proprietor inside pointing toward Robert, Ralph and Louise step forth and interrupt Honeyboy. When she moves to address Robert, Ralph interrupts her.

RALPH

Step aside, Louise. Your name Robert Johnson, fella, what makes them records in there?

Picking his guitar, eyeing Louise, who eyes him back, Robert nods affirmatively.

RALPH

We havin' a getback party tonight, but that

damn Graphonola inside's busted up an'—how's
that guitar sound there?

Ralph takes the guitar from Robert, who gazes at
Louise. The paunchy gentleman tunes the guitar while
talking.

RALPH

Louise an' I heard you can play. There be lotsa
folks comin', all the whiskey you want. Big
Ralph'll pay. You get there.

HONEYBOY

I's his partner Honeyboy—

RALPH

Out past Itta Bena, near a place called Three
Forks, ten o'clock.

ROBERT (to Louise)

Yeah. I'll get there. Say, you heard of Noah
Johnson?

LOUISE (playfully)

Maybe.

Ralph hands the guitar back to Robert, who plucks it
and lifts the box to his ear.

229. EXTERIOR. HOUSE PARTY. NIGHT.

A white clapboard house on the edge of a cotton field. A
similar house beside it, with three others scattered into
the field. People are moving inside and out; Robert can
be heard singing the end to "Terraplane."

ROBERT (singing) (off)

"I'm gonna mash down on yo' lil starter, an'
yo' spark plugs'll give me fire—"

Ralph drags his broken Victrola beneath a banner reading "GETBACK" and places it outside the party on the
porch.

230. INTERIOR. HOUSE PARTY. NIGHT

Robert keeps his enthusiastic throng dancing by beginning his next song forthwith. Honeyboy backs him unob-
trusively.

ROBERT (singing)

"I'm a steady rollin' man, I roll both night an'
day/ An' I haven't got no sweet woman, HOO!
boys, t'be rollin' thisaway—"

Louise dances over to Robert and rubs her posterior
against him. He pokes his guitar neck at the inviting
target.

231. EXTERIOR. PORCH. NIGHT.

Ralph is fixing the Victrola with a screwdriver.

ROBERT (singing) (off)

"I'm the man that row, with icicles hangin' on
the trees./ Y'hear me howlin', baby, HOO!
babe, down on my bended knee—"

Ralph moves to the window. Inside, the party is a success, and Ralph's wife strokes Robert's leg, enjoying the
party most of all.

FAST DISSOLVE.

232. INTERIOR. HOUSE PARTY. NIGHT.

Robert is singing for Louise now as the drunken atmosphere heightens. She rubs her crotch on seated Robert's shoulder.

ROBERT (singing)

"She the little Queen o' Spades, an' the men will not let her be./ Whenev' she make a spread ooo! cold chill run all over me—"

Ralph pauses in the doorway to behold the general scene. As Robert sticks his whiskey bottle into Louise's mouth, he grips his screwdriver and casually passes through.

233. EXTERIOR. BACK DOOR. NIGHT.

The inexpressive Ralph steps outside and walks toward a small toolshed.

ROBERT (singing) (off)

"Lil girl, I am a king, an' fair brown you is a queen./ Let's put our heads together so we can make our money green—"

234. INTERIOR. TOOLSHED. NIGHT.

Ralph casually examines a few wrenches and screwdrivers. He selects one of each, then takes a tiny glass bottle off the shelf and pockets it.

235. INTERIOR. HOUSE PARTY. NIGHT.

Robert performs one of his sweetest songs, with Louise caressing him from behind.

ROBERT (singing)

"From four till late I was wringin' my hands an'
cryin'./ I believe to my soul that your daddy's
Gulfport bound—"

Ralph strolls through again and goes out the front door,
glancing back impassively as the dancing and singing
continue.

236. EXTERIOR. PORCH. NIGHT.

Ralph walks back from the nearby hootch stand with a
soda bottle filled with whiskey. Beside the Victrola he
pours the tiny bottle's contents into the larger one.

ROBERT (singing) (off)

"From Memphis to Norfolk is a thirty-six hours'
drive./ A man is like a prisoner, an' he's never
satisfied—"

Louise steps outside. She puts her arm around Ralph,
who kneels while fixing the Victrola.

LOUISE

Ralph, honey, why ain't you inside dancin' with
me? How come, baby?

RALPH

Gotta fix this for ya first, doll. Can't dance anyway. You know me.

LOUISE

Can't dance? Since when? That boy inside
make anybody dance.

RALPH

We do our dancin' in the bedroom. Here, bring that sissy somethin' to drink. He's earned it. Now don't you be worryin' 'bout me.

ROBERT (singing) (off)

"When I leave this town I'm gonna bid you fair farewell/ An' when I return again you have a great long story to tell—"

Louise kisses Ralph and re-enters the house. He resumes his work while, looking through the window over his shoulder, we see Robert take the bottle and drink up.

FAST DISSOLVE.

237. INTERIOR. HOUSE PARTY. LATE NIGHT.

Robert's fast dance number has the action at a sizzling tempo. Standing now, he watches Louise bump and grind.

ROBERT (singing)

"Every time I'm walkin' down the street/ Some pretty mama, she start breakin' down with me./ Stuff I got'll bust your brains out ooo! It'll make you lose yo' mind—"

The rhythm is undeniable. Louise guzzles booze while lifting her skirt up her thighs. Robert smiles tentatively, as if bothered by something unclear to him.

ROBERT (singing)

"You know the Saturday night womens, now, like to ape an' clown./ Won't do nothin' but tear a good man's reputation down—"

Robert grimaces and clutches his stomach. Louise notices and takes hold of him, dancing. He tries to dance but cannot, so he keeps playing and singing, his pain concealed.

238. EXTERIOR. PORCH. LATE NIGHT.

Ralph gazes inside as Robert's fearsome performance continues. He sees the empty bottle at his feet.

> ROBERT (singing) (off)
>
> "PLEASE! stop breakin' down./ Stuff I got gonna bust yo' brains out HOO! make you lose your mind—"

He calmly returns to the Victrola as Louise steps outside.

> LOUISE
>
> C'mon, darlin', party's gonna be over soon. That boy's about had it.

> RALPH
>
> We paid him three bucks. He ain't done yet. I be in a minute—

FAST DISSOLVE.

239. INTERIOR. HOUSE PARTY. WEE HOURS.

With the guests dancing at a furious pace, a sweaty Robert suddenly shifts to a slower, unsteady rhythm. A wall clock reads two o'clock. Honeyboy is seen leaving for the night, so drunk he can hardly get through the door.

ROBERT (singing)

"Tell me, milk cow, what on earth is wrong
with you?/ Well, you have a lil new calf, an'
your milk is turnin' blue—"

Robert is in obvious pain. His legs unsteady, he performs desperately well. Louise is dancing seductively for
Robert, pouting and cupping her breasts, as Ralph
glances in through the window unnoticed. She swigs her
bottle, pours it over Robert's head and dances away to
another man.

ROBERT (singing)

"Now your calf is hungry, I believe he needs a
suck./ Well, but the milk is turnin' blue, I believe he's out of luck—"

Ralph lugs the Victrola inside. Robert looks to him
supplicatively. Ralph stares at him coldly, then turns
away. Louise dances toward Ralph as he sets the machine down in a corner.

ROBERT (singing)

"I feel like milkin' an' my cow won't come, I
feel like churnin', my milk won't turn./ I'm
cryin' 'Plea-HEASE! Don't do me wrong.'/ If you
see my milk cow baby now-how, PLEASE! drive
her home—"

Ralph is winding up the Victrola. Louise caresses him
and licks his ear. In the background, seen between
dancers, Robert's eyes are rolling backward, mouth
agape, for a chilling second. He sits, then quickly stands
up again.

ROBERT (singing)

"My milk cow been ramblin', hoo! for miles
around—"

Robert staggers two steps. He looks up strangely, scan-
ning the reeling, dimly lit room. A couple make love in a
dark corner. Leaning against the opposite wall from
Robert, seen between moving bodies, the devilman
scratches his balls. As Louise dances all over, Ralph casually selects a record. Now the devilman exits. Robert
steps back near the door.

ROBERT (singing)

"Well, can you suck on some other man's bull
cow in this strange man's town?"

240.   EXTERIOR. HOUSE PARTY. WEE HOURS.

Robert bangs violently into the doorway, then, throwing
down his guitar, tumbles over the porch outside. He
twists in the dust, stands, falls again. The crowd pours
out to find him yelping raspily on his hands and knees
like a rabid animal, kicking up clouds of dust. He races
to the far side of the moonlit yard and drops to his
hands and knees again in swirling clouds of dust. The
surrounding throng follows excitedly. A flash of ecstatic
Lavendar, jumping up and down on two good legs in
the shadows. A confusion of voices.

LAVENDAR

KNEEEEE-HIIIIIIIIIIIGHHH!!!

Robert scampers through billowing dust into the dark
field. Ralph stands in the window beside his Victrola,
watching. A Robert Johnson record is playing subtly.
The crowd starts toward Robert in the field, then drifts
back toward the music instead. Ralph and Louise are in
the window, kissing.

VICTROLA

"She got a phonograph, an' it won't say a lonesome word./ What evil have I done, what evil
has the poor girl heard?"

Robert stands in the plowed field, then collapses, alone.

FADE OUT.

FADE IN.

241. EXTERIOR. ROAD BESIDE FIELD. MORNING.

One hundred yards away, two elderly sharecroppers
stroll toward the camera alongside the cotton field. A
third is walking into the field toward Robert, inert, lying
in the dirt. The other two continue on, talking low.

CROPPER 1

Who the debil done it?

CROPPER 2

Lyons, like before.

CROPPER 1

Willie 'gain?

Distantly, in the background, the unidentifiable man
drags Robert to the road and lifts him upright.

CROPPER 2

Yeah. Got 'im to his hand an' knee. Stabbed 'im.
Cut open all his ches'. We watched it. Kid from
Hazlehurst—

DISSOLVE.

242. INTERIOR. ONE-ROOM SHACK. NOON.

A small room with painted peach wallpaper, patched with newspaper. Robert's head is a black dot in a bed of white. Seated at the foot of the bed beside a radio, drinking, is the devilman. Robert strains to speak. He is ignored.

ROBERT

How long I been here?

The devilman looks away, drinking. Then he stares at Robert.

ROBERT

Where's the doctor? When he come?

The devilman swigs his bottle and fiddles with the radio.

ROBERT

What's your name?

DEVILMAN

Tush Hogg. Doctor Tush Hogg.

ROBERT (eyes closed)

That ain't your name.

DEVILMAN (drinking)

Then what is?

ROBERT

Gimme a paper. I'll tell you.

The devilman drops a slip of paper into Robert's hand, then stands in the doorway looking outside. He flags down a pickup truck. Turning around, he sees Robert let go of his pencil, dead. He stares at the slip of paper.

CLOSEUP, paper: "Jesus Christ, my saver an redeemer"

243. EXTERIOR. ONE-ROOM SHACK. NOON.

The devilman steps outside, bearing Robert over to the waiting pickup truck. As he and the driver stretch the body out in the rear, one of the most ethereal recordings ever made is heard: Washington Phillips' 1927 "I Had a Good Father and Mother." It is also the most beautiful song in the film.

SUPER: "At the time of the poisoning, Don Law was searching for Robert throughout Mississippi, with an offer for him to sing in New York City at Carnegie Hall. But on August 16, 1938, Robert Johnson died, and was buried somewhere in the Delta in an unmarked grave."

The pickup truck drives up the dusty road with the lifeless body shifting about behind. The moving spiritual continues.

RECORDING

"I'm so glad Salvation is free, it is free for you an' me./ Now if we jus' only live with Jesus, how happy we could be—"

The melody heightens into a magically precious cooing, as the distant truck disappears in its own clouds of dust.

DISSOLVE.

244. PHOTOGRAPH OF ROBERT JOHNSON.

A photograph of Robert Johnson taken in a studio in the 1930s. He is a handsome young black man, wearing a new suit and tie and dark fedora, his battered guitar on his lap. Smiling innocently, tentatively, he leans forward slightly, eyes staring downward in different directions.

RECORDING

"I know this whole round world do not love me nohow, an' it is on the count of sin/ But I'm so thankful God is able for to give me many friends—"

FADE TO BLACK.

SUPER: "End"

SUPER: "Love in Vain"

Robert Johnson Studio Portrait
Copyright 1989 Mimosa Records Productions, Inc.
Used by Permission. All Rights Reserved.

"Jake's Place," a jook joint lost in the fields between Morgan City and Itta Bena, Mississippi. Near Three Forks, where Robert Johnson last played. Interior walls painted randomly in different dark shades, a polka-dotted ceiling, larger-than-life carnal images, and a sign reading "No bad language, please."

A tiny white clapboard Baptist church on the edge of a cottonfield, shaded by a chinaberry tree. Six miles north of Clarksdale, Mississippi, it was razed in 1980. Inside, the local voodoo conjurer (see note 33:1) kept his office in the rear. *"Good with two magics better than one—"*

A crossroads on Charlie's Trace (see note 36:1), a short-cut between a Mississippi River landing and the hills, a few miles below Clarksdale. This dirt swath, allegedly cut by a Choctaw Indian, was the route of marauding outlaws in the early 1800s, and of itinerant bluesmen in the early 1900s.

In Friars Point, Mississippi, the author was referred to Dutch Carter, a 93 year-old former bartender with vivid memories of his friend Charley Patton. When approached, the old man said he wasn't Dutch Carter, and hadn't heard of him. Two days later, after learning of his visitor's purpose from people in town, he changed his mind and generously provided his recollection of 1930s riverside jooks and barrelhouses. Then he was asked why he'd first denied being Dutch Carter. "That's the problem," he complained. "Since I come here 40 years ago, everyone calls me Dutch Carter. But my name's Willie McGee."

Fringed by dark trees on tufted banks, the Sunflower River winds through Clarksdale, a typical Delta town with flat terrain, far horizons, and vast surrounding cottonfields. The former cotton processing and musical hub is now the home of the Delta Blues Museum.

Levees were notorious for shielding not only riverside towns from flood tides, but criminals and "sinners" from the forces of law and morality as well. On the far side of the levee, every sort of character acted out his darkest fantasies in an atmosphere of sinister, oblivious dread. Insipid attempts to control ways of the soul resulted in warning signs like this one on the levee road near Friars Point.

A cobblestoned street and storefronts, scarcely changed since the early 1900s like many Delta towns, beside the railroad tracks in Itta Bena. Bluesmen were often encouraged to perform outside these local shops to attract customers. But due to the Mississippi "dry state" laws, which supplanted the repealed national statute prohibiting hard liquor after 1933, a liquor store such as the one above would not have been in business back in Robert Johnson's day.

With its stark skeletal cypresses and weeping willows, the Yazoo River (Choctaw for "River of Death") starts near Greenwood and runs along U.S. Highway 61 to Redwood, where it diverges and ceases its flow just north of Vicksburg.

Notes

Scene number in parentheses.

(1)

1. "During a peaceful lull in the Afro-American church service, after a song has been sung and the church is resting, or after the deacon has prayed and led the first hymn and everyone sits wondering what will come, then an ethereal humming arises among the women: the *Lining Hymn*, or the *Church-House Moan*. A spiritual pure and ineffable, the strong, sorrowful moan moves through the room like an ancestral breeze stirring placid waters. An older woman in the rear starts tapping a quick staccato rhythm with her toe to set the tempo for all that follows. The deacon and congregation adorn the air with unexpected harmonies as the minister leans forward and, in a deep despairing voice that tugs at the heart, raises the first line of his sermon." Alan Lomax, *Recorded Anthology of American Music* (New York: New World Records, 1977), liner notes.

2. A vanishing custom among Southern Afro-American people. By swinging the ax through the threatening winds or using it to chop up the ground, one is able then to "chop the storm in two" and so stop it. Others stick a blade in the ground to "split the cloud," or simply place an ax in a corner of the house. "The use of the ax as an antidote to the storm is significant, since the West African god of thunder and lightning, *Shango*, is an ax." What has survived is folk custom, devoid of African theological background, re-enacting an original mythological image. Albert J. Raboteau, *Slave Religion* (New York: Oxford, 1978), p. 81.

3. "SUPER" is a shortened form of "superimposition," in this case referring to the appearance of text over the visual image.

4. While his mother and second stepfather Willie "Dusty" Willis labored on the Abbay-Leatherman plantation in nearby Commerce, Robert Johnson grew to manhood in and around Robinsonville, a

small (population 150) Mississippi cotton community forty miles south of Memphis. Enrolled under his first stepfather's pseudonym of Spencer at the Indian Creek School in Commerce, Robert learned the identity of his natural father—one of his mother's lovers —and began to introduce himself as Robert *Johnson*. There were four *jook joints* (see below) in the Robinsonville area, where Robert would steal away with his jew's harp or harmonica to listen to Willie Brown, Charley Patton, Ernest "Whisky Red" Brown and, upon his arrival in June 1930, Eddie "Son" House.

(2)

1. Friars Point (population 988 in 1930), sitting in the shadow of a flood wall blocking the Mississippi River from view, was abandoned as a county seat in 1930 because of the menacing river, which had swallowed every major river town established since 1830. A forsaken community today, old-timers gather outside a dry goods store to fill the desolate air with recollected images of traveling singers from W. C. Handy to Charley Patton, those native and adopted sons who once drew masses of delighted black folk and tolerant whites to local street corners half a century ago. Few of the living express any concern or need for the African homeland; fewer still remember their elders' reflections, told as truth with touches of fantasy, documenting remedies for the repressed horrors of spiritual displacement.

2. Willie Johnson was a singer of religious songs from Marlin, Texas, who, like several of his contemporaries, was assigned the nickname "Blind" for his recordings and came to be known as Blind Willie Johnson. His songs, even when taken from hymnals, were profoundly expressive of his personal poetic vision, with a vibrancy of tone and a vividness of image. On a farm near the Brazos River where he was born around 1902, Willie's stepmother threw a pan of lye in his face when he was seven to get even with his father for a beating, thereby leaving the boy sightless for life. He sang in the streets of small cotton towns in southern Texas and came to Dallas in 1927, where his future wife and singing partner Angeline followed him as he sang "If I Had My Way I'd Tear This Building Down" until he noticed her. Sounding like a man many years older than he was, Willie rendered his first recordings in Dallas that same year and became one of the most successful recording artists in the South for several years. When his record company went bankrupt in 1932, he dropped from sight and never recorded again. Caught one night in 1949 in a house fire in Beaumont, Texas, he and Angeline managed to douse the flames and then, having no money to go elsewhere, they climbed back

into their charred, drenched bed and went to sleep. Willie soon came down with pneumonia while continuing to sing on the chilly streets. When he finally sought help at a local hospital, he was told that no blind people were allowed in, so he returned to his devastated home and died within days. Some of Blind Willie Johnson's most beloved songs were "Jesus Make Up My Dying Bed," "Trouble Soon Be Over," "Lord, I Just Can't Keep from Crying," "Motherless Children Have a Hard Time," and "Nobody's Fault but Mine." Samuel Charters, *Blind Willie Johnson, 1927–1930* (New York: Folkways Records, 1965), liner notes.

3. Sharecroppers were tenant farmers in the racially corrupt agricultural system that dominated the South until the Afro-American diaspora of the 1930s and '40s. Kept helplessly compliant through official programs of economic and educational deprivation, the black sharecroppers wallowed in permanent debt, owing to imaginary, grossly inflated fees charged by white landowners. The blacks were wise to such cruelty but were powerless to do anything about it, outside of moving into urban industrial centers for a different sort of squalid self-mockery.

4. After a recollection offered by Shad Hall. Harold Courlander, *A Treasury of Afro-American Folklore* (New York: Crown Publishers, 1976).

(3)

1. *Jook joints,* sometimes called *barrelhouses,* as essential to the Afro-American reality in the Delta as the Church, sheltered the lunar visage of the Sunday religious service, the Saturday night dance. The word "jook" seems to be derived from any of several sources in West African culture, such as *joog,* which suggests "to agitate" or "shake up," or *yuka,* from the Vili Congo dialect, connoting "making a noise, to hit or beat." Typically no more than a primitive, one-room shanty, the jook would be found in some remote terrestrial zone far from the church and even farther from the law (the bootlegger-proprietors often paid for police immunity). People went there to drink, dance, play or listen to music, gamble, look for a fight, look for a lover, and so on. Beer was served in tin cups, whiskey and gin in cans or the same tin cups; mugs weren't used "because the people would commit mayhem, tear people's heads up with those things—rough places they were," reflects John Shines. "When you were playing in a place like that," Mr. Shines continues, "you just sit back there with the dancing on a cane-bottomed chair, just rear back and cut loose." Live music gradually disappeared from most Delta jooks with the advent of the jukebox, or *vendor,* but several jooks with live music may be

found in northwestern Mississippi today, such as Jake's Place, a visionary sheet metal hovel lost in a cotton field somewhere south of Itta Bena.

2. Willie Brown was one of the greatest of Delta bluesmen. A brilliant, forceful guitarist, he is remembered for his accompaniment of Charley Patton and Son House, and for his recordings of "Future Blues" and "M & O Blues." Brown was born around the turn of the century and spent much of his life in Robinsonville, where he came into contact with Robert Johnson. Robert copied his mentor's exaggerated plucking technique but avoided Brown's tendency to break guitar strings. Listed as William Brown, he recorded for Alan Lomax and the Library of Congress in 1942, and may be heard today on album AFS L59.

3. Eddie "Son" House was born near Riverton, Mississippi, in 1898, and was raised across the river from Vicksburg in Louisiana. He was brought up "in church," in opposition to the Devil-courting bluesmen and their followers. "It always made me mad to see a man with a guitar, singing these blues and things," he reflected many years later. House became one of the most powerful and emotional singers in the Delta, working regularly with the likes of Brown, Patton and, later, Robert Johnson. His 1930 recordings of "Preachin' the Blues," "My Black Mama" and "Delta Blues" are monuments of the genre, as are his 1942 recordings of "Jinx Blues," "Special Rider Blues" and "Depot Blues" for the Library of Congress. After receiving but forty dollars from his record company for his 1930 releases, and then just a bottle of Coca-Cola from Alan Lomax for his work in 1942, Son disappeared from view until the 1964 Newport Folk Festival, with his wealth of talent and spirit largely undiminished. He made a score of excellent new recordings before retiring once more, to Detroit this time, where he died in 1988.

4. In 1903, W. C. Handy was touring the Delta with his orchestra when, in the Mississippi town of Tutwiler, not far from Charley Patton's home in Drew, "a lean, loose-jointed Negro had commenced plucking a guitar beside me . . . as he played, he pressed a knife on the strings of the guitar," and performed "the weirdest music" Handy had ever heard. This was the first documentation of slide or bottleneck guitar technique, an art form in itself today after generations of development by Delta, Hawaiian, and country-western guitar players. Using a blade, piece of pipe, glass bottle or bone, the musician slides his tool up and down the guitar neck to bend and extend various chords or, in the parlance of the Southern Afro-American, to make the guitar *talk*. Technically rather simple to learn, Son House was a master slide guitarist by 1930 although

he'd been too "churchified" to learn guitar at all until 1927, less than three years before.

5. Delta musicians would frequently expand the boundaries of a given song, or render it unidentifiable altogether, by interchanging verses and versions of different songs within the basic melodic-rhythmic structure of the original. This was done spontaneously, either in solo or group performance, and called for a mind like a deranged computer bank. Since a typical jook joint song performance often lasted twenty minutes or more (until a trancelike momentum had been achieved), a jook entertainer would be hard pressed to please his demanding audience. Once a singer faltered, it wouldn't be long before another singer challenged him to an improvisational duel on the spot, or simply replaced him.

6. In this scene, Son House and Willie Brown are depicted trading verses to different songs while performing the same song together. Son borrows from Charley Patton's "Screamin' and Hollerin' the Blues" ("Girl, my mama's gettin' old, her head is turnin' gray./ Don't you know it'll break her heart, know my livin' this-a-way?"), while Willie shouts out his own "M & O Blues" ("An' I asked her, 'How 'bout it?' Lord, an' she said, 'All right,'/ But she never showed up at the shack last night . . .").

(4)

1. Robert Johnson was a devilishly handsome Afro-American man with a markedly youthful mien who, according to accounts of those who knew him, almost always appeared meticulously groomed. John Shines, who traveled extensively with Robert for a few weeks prior to Robert's death, recollected, "We'd be on the road for days and days, no money and sometimes not much food, let alone a decent place to spend the night, playing on dusty streets or inside dirty places of the sort you played in in those times, and as I'd catch my breath and see myself looking like a *dog*, there'd be Robert, all clean as can be, looking like he's just stepped out of *church*. Never did nothing to himself any more than me, neither. . . ."

2. *Hootch* was one of several slang terms for illegally distilled corn whiskey sold throughout the Delta and elsewhere. In 1930 the popularity of various types of bootleg liquor among Southern black people was due not so much to federal Prohibition but rather to the Mississippi "dry state" laws, which supplanted the repealed national statute against hard liquor after 1933.

3. Goat is a character derived by the author from two people who actually lived and performed music in the South around the time of Robert Johnson. Essentially, this character is drawn from the re-

markable singer and songwriter Tommy Johnson, who was born around 1896 in Terry, Mississippi, and died in 1956 in Crystal Springs. Recently established as a distant relative of Robert Johnson by his biographer David Evans, Tommy Johnson, a strange primitive genius, affected his generation of musicians more than anyone except Charley Patton. It was from Patton, in fact, that Johnson received his primary musical schooling, during the intense musical scene around the Drew, Mississippi, plantations from about 1912 to 1918. Johnson was famous for his wondrous vocal technique; instead of the customary chant, he *yodeled* several of his songs, swallowing his words to obliterate whatever literal value they might have had (which was the case with most Afro-American singers, who utilized their acquired language for *imaginal* ends, more than literal). However renowned he might have been for his music, Johnson was equally famous for his weird drinking habits. One of the greatest drunkards of all time, he would drink anything—denatured alcohol, shoe polish, petroleum extracts—anything that would get him high. Addicted to Sterno, a jellied cooking fuel, he drank several cans a day right up to his peaceful death at the age of sixty. "He believed in it," says his brother Mager. Johnson was alleged to have been an agent of the Devil, a rumor he encouraged to enhance his personal legend and popularity. Among the fifteen surviving Tommy Johnson songs on record ("Louisiana Blues" has never been found), the most celebrated are his "Canned Heat Blues," "Maggie Campbell Blues," "Big Road Blues," and the incomparable, hallucinatory "Cool Drink of Water." David Evans, *Tommy Johnson* (London: Studio Vista, 1971).

4. One of the many songs recorded during the 1930s on the "jake leg" theme. The emotionally urgent version by Poor Boy Lofton, sung here by Lavendar, documents the paralysis and other afflictions suffered by countless Delta black people who drank a bootlegged ginger extract as an inexpensive whiskey substitute. Also referred to as the "limber leg."

5. As a young boy, Robert Johnson would return from a day in the cotton fields, head down behind his stepfather's cart, his figure increasingly covered with dust. The inevitable nickname "Dusty"—a nemesis to Robert, being the tag worn by his second stepfather as well—followed.

6. Robert's mother, Julia Ann Majors, was married to Charles Dodds, Jr., a well-respected farmer and landowner. A personal conflict with two powerful white businessmen forced Dodds to flee Mississippi for Memphis in 1907, where he assumed the name of Spencer. Julia stayed behind with two of her daughters in Hazlehurst. On May 8, 1911, Robert Johnson was born to Julia Dodds

and Noah Johnson, a sharecropper with whom Julia had had an affair during her husband's enforced absence. Despite recent claims to the contrary, Johnny Shines and others who knew Robert assert that Robert never met his father, and from time to time swung between a sullen disregard for him and an obsessive concern for his whereabouts.

(6)

1. Willie is singing a verse from Son's "Jinx Blues," one of young Robert's favorites ("You know the blues ain't nothin' but a low-down, shakin' achin' chill./ Well, if you ain't had 'em, honey, I hope you never will . . . "). Copyright 1965 by Sondick Music Company.

2. In his preadolescent years, while he was still known as Robert Spencer, Robert committed himself to music by taking up the jew's harp. This instrument was soon replaced by the harmonica, which had been introduced to him by his best friend. Upon making the transition to guitar a few years later, Robert fashioned a rack for his harmonica out of string and baling wire, then worked out songs for his voice and instrumental accompaniment. Leroy Carr's "How Long, How Long Blues" was used early on as one of Robert's instructional models.

3. Eventually, Son prevented such accidents by wrapping an oily rag around his hand for protection from the sharp glass bottleneck.

(8)

1. Charley Patton was the pre-eminent Delta bluesman of his day, a man whose shamanistic spirit and ways defined his musical idiom aesthetically and culturally, and encouraged its growth. Born near Edwards, Mississippi, in 1891, Patton was almost a generation older than most of his contemporaries. Physically small, he was a strange-looking blend of white, black, but primarily Indian blood; dressed like an urchin in his snug suit and bow tie, Patton seemed to be a Rimbaudian image incarnate or, from another angle, "he looked kind of like a Puerto Rican," according to Howlin' Wolf. "He was illiterate, and spent his time in total idleness, inevitably drunk. His friends remember him as a troublemaker, a runt with a big mouth and quick feet. Patton was extremely cheap with whatever money he had, would pledge eternal love to any woman gullible enough to listen, and was a notorious tyrant with his eight-odd common-law wives, beating them regularly. Since he was a favorite with the whites as well as the blacks, Patton passed easily between antipodal worlds while hardly ever putting in an honest day's labor. 'That's the way he lived, eating out of the white folks'

kitchen,' says Son House. He must have been the very archetype of
the 'bad plantation nigger' around the Will Dockery and Joe Kirby
plantations, where he spent most of his time. His only child, China
Lu, disavowed him.

"Patton's hoard of imitators all lacked some of his virtues. No
one compared with him for colorful, exciting and shamelessly lewd
public performances, nor did any of his musical peers leave so extensive a studio portrait. His repertoire was broader than the typical Mississippian's, encompassing hard Delta blues, ragtime,
'covers' of popular songs, and folk blues or ballads. His crude
lyricism offers local-color imagery unmatched by any other bluesman. His diction and vocal techniques were so unusual and idiosyncratic that purists like Son House scorned him for rendering his
songs unintelligible," which they probably were when sung most
successfully. Although Patton's music indicates a good grasp of
melody and harmony, his genius was principally rhythmic, with
rhythm assuming such importance in each work that it ultimately
became the work itself. Owing to the nature of his singing
rhythms, Patton's guitar instrumentation took on the cadence of
speech, most notably so in "Spoonful," one of his landmark recordings. Other great recordings of his are "Pony Blues," "Tom Rushen
Blues," "Some These Days I'll Be Gone," "High Water Everywhere," and "Pea Vine Blues." He also recorded religious songs,
under the pseudonym of Elder J. J. Hadley. Three months after
recording with his wife Bertha Lee in New York City, Charley Patton died in Holly Ridge, Mississippi, of heart failure. Nick Perls,
Stephen Calt, et al., *Charley Patton—Founder of the Delta Blues*
(New York: Yazoo Records, L-1020), liner notes. John Fahey,
Charley Patton (London: Studio Vista, 1970).

(10)

1. "Long, Hot Summer Days" is a work song recorded in Texas in
1939 by John A. and Ruby T. Lomax. Sung in the fields by Clyde
Hill and his fellow prisoners at Clemens State Farm in Brazoria,
this recording can be found on a Library of Congress LP,
AAFS L3.

2. The only people to accompany Charley Patton on record were
his wife Bertha Lee (see note 29:1), Willie Brown, and the Clarksdale fiddler Henry Sims. Sims, who later recorded for the Library
of Congress with Muddy Waters, was an articulate primitive on
fiddle who complemented Patton perfectly. The rough tones of
Sims's inimitable fiddle are due to his instrument being homemade, or in an absurd state of disrepair. As a singer he possessed a
distinctly mournful quality, which went well with his playing.

Among his recordings are "Farrell Blues," "Come Back Corrina," "Tell Me Man Blues," and "Be True Be True Blues," all with a drunken Charley Patton in dubious support. Don Kent, *Patton, Sims, and Bertha Lee* (New York: Herwin Records, 1977), liner notes.

3. H. C. Speir was the white owner of a Jackson music store who acted as a talent scout for the major record companies in the "race" and "hillbilly" markets. He would find artists who were already popular in the black community, make test recordings of them in his store, send these to the companies for approval, and then make the arrangements for the accepted artists to get to the studios to record. Born in Mississippi in 1895, Speir grew up liking the black music he heard all around him, which helped make his taste quite close to the black audiences of his day. His sole criterion for selecting a good singer was his personal taste, not the singer's popularity among blacks. Speir claimed he never could tell a good blues singer, as some sounded excellent in person but poor on record, or vice versa. He was also unaware that many blues lyrics were metaphorical, and took all the songs he heard at face value. Speir was a friendly man who was interested in music as much for pleasure as for profit. The Jackson area's finest musicians would frequent his store to buy strings and picks, or just chat. Some of the musicians who came to Speir's store and were "discovered" by Speir were Tommy Johnson, Charley Patton, Willie Brown, Skip James, and Ishman Bracey. Evans, op. cit., pp. 45–46.

4. "This Old World's in a Hell of a Fix" was the subject of a sermon given by Rev. Dr. J. McPherson, also known as Black Billy Sunday, in 1931. A recording of this sermon was made and is preserved today on Biograph Records (BLP-12027).

(11)

1. Goat is singing Tommy Johnson's extraordinary "Cool Drink of Water." The verses of the song are disconnected but traditional, and can be found scattered among many other country blues performances. The music of the song is startling. Almost half of the vocal, including the "Lord, Lordy Lord" primal refrain, is sung in falsetto, creating the overall impression of a chant somewhere in between a field holler and an Alpine yodel. Yet the instrumentation is unique, and quite sophisticated, with the guitars perfectly integrated into the vocal line. The 1928 recording was released on Victor 21279. Ibid., pp. 48–49.

2. An Afro-American spiritual dating back to the days of slavery, recently recorded for cultures worldwide by the Rolling Stones.

(12)

1. After his 1928 recording session Tommy Johnson never re-corded again. His records were popular and sold very well, but a strange misunderstanding coupled with Johnson's perpetual drunk-enness ended his recording career. What apparently happened was this: the Mississippi Sheiks recorded a song taken from Johnson's own "Big Road Blues" and made an enormous hit out of it. The Victor Company, which owned "Big Road Blues," sued the Okeh Company, which recorded the Sheiks, and a settlement was made. Johnson, the composer of the song, was included in the settlement, but he was drunk at the time and wound up with less than he de-served. And somehow he believed that he had sold his right to re-cord ever again. His brother thought the same thing. "He drank so much he sold his rights, and he couldn't put out no more records," said the Rev. LeDell Johnson. "According to his records he didn't get nothing much. See, when Tom get broke, he would sell any-thing to get a drink of whisky or a drink of alcorub or anything that'd bring on drunk." Ibid., p. 68.

(16)

1. A vestige of Afro-American slavery days and, then again, of ancestral times in the African homeland, the *one-string* is the most primitive musical instrument associated with the Delta blues. Whether constructed for portability from a discarded two-by-four or simply nailed to a wall, the one-string is made with a steel wire strung between two nails three feet apart and raised above the two-by-four or wall by bridges; one bridge is a stone or wooden block, the other a hollow vial or pill bottle fastened beneath a resonator fashioned from an empty paint can. The player of the in-strument beats the wire near the resonator with a whittled stick while sliding a half-pint whiskey flask up and down the wire to alter tones. Plucking is often used in place of the percussion. Frederick Usher, *One-String Blues* (Santa Monica: Takoma Rec-ords, 1960), liner notes.

2. The Piney Woods of Mississippi is an irregular triangle of forest land whose landscape of stumps, ghost towns left by the lumber trade, and hastily reforested tracts tells its story. Until lumbering built a few fair-sized towns out of the wilderness it was a pioneer territory; by 1930, with the woods ravaged and the poorly built mill houses rotting, it had become pioneer country once more. Like all pioneers, the Afro-American people of the Piney Woods were economically poor, politically unpredictable, and in a constant state of transition. With the geographic and economic character of

the region losing its meaning among its inhabitants, the Piney Woods assumed an ill-defined but widespread mythical character. Federal Writers' Project, Works Progress Administration, *Mississippi—A Guide to the Magnolia State* (New York: Hastings House, 1938), p. 6.

(18)

1. Five miles west on the graveled road from Robinsonville, Commerce (population 50 in 1930) was once a rival of Memphis for the river trade before becoming a plantation anchored by the big house built upon a large Indian burial mound. Richard Abbay first bought the land from the Chickasaw tribe in 1832, but the ravenous Mississippi flood tide destroyed the settlement by the time of the Civil War. The rebuilt Abbay-Leatherman plantation bordered both sides of the road from Robinsonville with its commissaries and planted fields. The main house was not constructed directly upon the Indian mound because of the owner's aversion to touching a mound "full of the dead." From the top of the mound, which rises now behind the house, De Soto had his first glimpse of the river that was to be his grave, in 1541. Ibid., p. 316.

2. Lonnie Johnson was one of the first blues guitarists to achieve commercial stardom. His work bordered on jazz and he was comfortable within each idiom. Born in New Orleans, probably in 1894, Johnson first achieved proficiency on the violin before he took up the guitar in 1917. He was an immediate success upon the release of his first recordings in 1926; by the time the Depression ended the first phase of his recording career in 1932, Johnson had produced 130 sides, more than any male blues singer of the period. His fame was unparalleled within the blues universe and his influence on other musicians very pronounced. Young Robert Johnson not only bore the Lonnie Johnson imprint on guitar but was known to go around claiming kinship to the star. Long interpreted as idiosyncratic evidence of his egotistical nature, Robert's claims concerning the older musician have been corroborated recently by researchers.

3. And, conversely, Son House learned the main tricks on Robert Johnson. The younger man's ultimate influence on his "mentor" House is generally overlooked.

4. In truth, Robert did not make any commercial recordings of any kind until November 1936.

5. Scrapper Blackwell, born Francis Black, was a celebrated black recording artist known for his brilliant guitarmanship, particularly in tandem with his equally celebrated partner, Leroy Carr.

(19)

1. The shimmy-she-wa-wa was a popular dance of the period. "They did that some way like that, you know, with their knees," remembers the Rev. Rubin Lacy, a bluesman once himself. "That's the reason I say it's all coming back. Ain't nothing but what you see them do now: whole lot of shaking going on." Evans, op. cit., p. 40.

(20)

1. "There's No Use Lovin'," one of Lonnie Johnson's earliest recordings (1926). Johnson plays the piano here, occasionally giving way to a whining siren. On Mamlish Records, number S-3807.

(21)

1. Moon Lake, located two and a half miles west of Lula, Mississippi (see Scene 108).

(22)

1. Taken from the woodcarved epitaph of an unknown slave. Harold Courlander, *A Treasury of Afro-American Folklore* (New York: Crown Publishers, 1976), p. 280.

2. Ike Zinnerman was a friend of Robert Johnson's from Grady, Alabama, who spent many a night teaching the younger man (in reality, only a few years separated them) blues guitar techniques. Born at the turn of the century, Zinnerman claimed that he mastered the guitar in a "boneyard" at midnight while sitting atop tombstones. Robert accompanied the bluesman before developing confidence enough to perform alone.

3. Erich Neumann, *The Origins and History of Consciousness* (Princeton, N.J.: Princeton University Press, 1954), p. 159. A literal instance of the essentially mythological character of Robert Johnson's life experiences and fate.

4. "Shorty George" is a traditional folk blues motif sung by black inmates on the Southwestern and Southern penal farms. The title is derived from a slang term given the train that brings the prisoners' family, friends and female visitors from the outside world. The version familiar to the author was sung by Smith Casey in 1939 at the Clemens State Farm in Brazoria, Texas, as a dirge for a dead comrade. The rest of the song as follows:

> *Yes, he died on the road,*
> *Yes, he died on the road,*
> *Had no money to pay his boa'd.*

Ahhhhhhhh, he was a friend of mine,
Yes, he was a friend of mine;
Every time I think now, just can't keep from cryin'.

I . . . . I stole away an' cried,
Yes, stole away an' cried;
Never had no money, now I wasn't satisfied.

Mmmmmmmmmm, wonder what's the matter now?
Lord, what is the matter now? . . .

Recorded for the Library of Congress by John A. and Ruby T. Lomax, and found on LP AFS L4.

(23)

1. Abstract spiritual systems find manifold ways to work on a human being's naked soul. In moments of weakness or personal stress, blues singers were particularly susceptible to fits of guilt in their shadowy corner of the Baptist subculture. Incidents such as the one occurring here in Ike's shack were not so uncommon, perhaps, to Delta life.

(25)

1. From the Tennessee border to the north, to the Louisiana line along the southern end, U. S. Highway 61 runs the entire length of 335 miles between Mississippi's state lines. It passes through the state's great alluvial plain, the extensive flat land colloquially known as the Delta, with its sluggish rivers, lakes and bayous. During the nineteenth century slave ships landed near Natchez to deposit their human cargo for processing; the Africans were fed, clothed, and taught a few English words, then they were sold on a block that stood on what is now US 61. During the 1930s the cotton and lumber industries made good use of the thoroughfare, which connected major trading centers such as Memphis, Clarksdale, Vicksburg, Natchez and Baton Rouge. Once emptied of their load, transport trucks would pick up sharecroppers needing a ride to town or the next plantation.

(27)

1. Robert is singing a song written and recorded by John Hurt, professionally known as Mississippi John Hurt, one of the most beloved of Delta recording artists. "Hurt was a *songster* more than a bluesman, since his repertoire covered folk ballads, ragtime tunes, and popular love songs as much as blues. Born in 1894, in the Carroll County area of Mississippi where he was to spend his whole

life, Hurt disappeared after his successful 1928 recording sessions, only to be rediscovered in 1963 when Tom Hoskins played Hurt's recording 'Avalon Blues' ("Avalon's my hometown, always on my mind . . ."), then went to Avalon, Mississippi, and found John Hurt there, waiting very patiently for him." Along with "Avalon Blues," "Louis Collins," "See See Rider," "Frankie" and "Candy Man Blues," "Got the Blues, Can't Be Satisfied" was one of his best efforts ("I said, 'Baby, what makes you act this-a-way?'/ Said I won't miss a thing she gives away." Copyright 1963 Wynwood Music Company, Inc.). John Hurt died in Grenada, Mississippi, in November 1966, at the age of seventy-three. Mike Leadbitter, *Nothing but the Blues* (London: Hanover Books, 1971), pp. 245–46.

(29)

1. Bertha Lee Pate, later Bertha Lee Joiner, was the last of Charley Patton's common-law wives. She joined Patton sometime after his 1929 recording sessions and, despite a minimum of natural singing skills, she performed with him regularly until his death in 1934. When Patton's own skills were in rapid decline, she went with him to New York City for his last sessions and cut a few records of her own: "Yellow Bee," "Mind Reader Blues," "Oh, Death" and "Troubled 'Bout My Mother." When interviewed for information about her legendary husband years after his death, Bertha Lee remembered only that Charley Patton played the guitar. She died in 1975 at the age of seventy-three. Fahey, op. cit., p. 16. Kent, op. cit., liner notes.

2. "Running Wild Blues" is, correctly speaking, no blues at all; rather, it is one of Charley Patton's square dance or hoedown numbers, perfect for street performance. The song has a Cajun flavor due to the Henry Sims fiddle part, which cavorts drunkenly over Patton's "boomchang" guitar. The lyrics are interesting for being nonsensical, almost unintelligible, creating a comical flood of absurdly repetitive images. It was recorded by Patton in 1929. Perls, Calt, et al., op. cit.

3. "Shake It and Break It" seems to have come out of the ragtime tradition, being similar to Bill Moore's "Barbershop Rag." The Rev. Gary Davis recorded a version of the song much closer to its ragtime roots, while Walter "Buddy Boy" Hawkins (see Scene 137) stayed closer to Patton's interpretation with his "Snatch It and Grab It," recorded with a soused Patton narrating the performance in the background.

(31)

1. Although Charley Patton was strictly an entertainer, not a social prophet in any sense, his songs frequently reflected the immediate sociohistorical reality he was a part of. "Mississippi Bo Weavil Blues" is a case in point: a funny song, it nevertheless documents the anxiety and physical hardship caused by the late 1920s onslaught of the boll weevil, a pest that devastated the cotton crop down South mercilessly. Black sharecroppers were badly hurt by the boll weevil, yet the songs written about the phenomenon reveal a fascination with the clever survival instincts of the insect. Patton's version directly compares the plight of the boll weevil with the plight of the average Delta Afro-American ("Bo weavil, bo weavil, where your native home, Lordy?/ Most anywhere they raisin' cotton an' corn, Lordy").

2. The verbal art known as the *dozens,* fundamentally a ritual of insult, has played a peculiarly essential role in Afro-American reality. Taking the form of verbal dueling, the dozens involves symmetrical relationships in which two or more people are free to insult each other, and each other's ancestors and relatives, either directly or indirectly. The mother is a favorite, but not invariable, target. A group of onlookers is generally present to comment upon the performance of each player, judge their abilities, incite them, urge them on. Although the dozens can end in physical violence, this is not the planned or preferred climax; the object of the contest is to withstand the temptation to violence by maintaining one's composure sufficiently to triumph by the rules, which value verbal facility, originality, ingenuity and humor. Lawrence W. Levine, *Black Culture and Black Consciousness* (New York: Oxford University Press, 1977), pp. 344–58.

(33)

1. *Conjure* is a theoretical and practical system stemming from African and Afro-American culture that makes sense of the mysterious and inexplicable occurrences of life. Like Christianity, conjure is a system of belief, a way of perceiving the world so that people are placed in the context of another world no less "real" than the ordinary one. Both attempt to locate the cause of irrational suffering. Not only is conjure a theory for explaining the mysteries of evil, but it is a practice as well for doing something about it. Because the conjuror has the power to "fix" and to remove "fixes," to harm and to cure, it is possible to locate the source of misfortune and control it. Thus the conjuror, as a man of power, has enjoyed since slavery a measure of authority in the Afro-American commu-

nity directly proportional to belief in his power. Certain conjurors are known to have offices in various churches around the Mississippi Delta to this day. Raboteau, op. cit., pp. 275–88.

2. The efficiency of the conjuror is rooted in his ability to "charm" his client, or to counteract another charm. The nature of such charismatic power is manifested physically by various *hands* or *mojos* selected or devised by the conjuror, whose stock in trade includes pins, bones, bottles, reptiles, insects, horsehair, roots and herbs. Graveyard dirt is considered particularly potent. It is also believed that each charm possesses a spirit. Consequently, some charms are moistened with liquor to strengthen their power by strengthening their spirits.

(34)

1. Most people who recall Charley Patton associate "Pony Blues" with him. According to John Fahey, it was his best-selling record and his most frequently requested song in live performances. One of Patton's "wives," Minnie Franklin of Merigold, Mississippi, reports that he was singing "Pony Blues" when she met him in 1924, but the song was probably much older. In the 1929 recording, Patton's idiosyncratic, galloping rhythms are evident with lyrics taken randomly from his kaleidoscopic storehouse of blues stanzas. Jeff Todd Titon, *Early Downhome Blues* (Chicago: University of Illinois Press, 1977), pp. 67–69.

(35)

1. According to John Shines, Robert was an avid moviegoer who favored Westerns and Clark Gable pictures.

(36)

1. Charlie's Trace, a dirt swath cut through fields and wilderness a few miles below Clarksdale, is alleged to have been made by a Choctaw Indian. The trail was a short cut from Sunflower Landing on the Mississippi River to a spot in the hills twelve miles south of Charleston, Mississippi. It was often the route of outlaws who marauded through this region in the early 1800s.

(37)

1. Blind Lemon Jefferson was born in the summer of 1897 in Couchman, Texas, about seventy-five miles from Dallas. He was born blind and, denied an education, was forced to earn a living early on as an itinerant singer. After playing and singing on the

streets of nearby Wortham he started his lifelong travels, and by the time he was twenty Lemon was singing for country dances and parties throughout the South. Before the start of World War I, he and Huddie Ledbetter (better known as Leadbelly) traveled and sang together in the Dallas area; Leadbelly went to prison and Lemon found local renown. At first, however, singing wasn't enough: he also wrestled for money in Dallas theaters, billed as a blind novelty wrestler. He did much of his singing in brothels, drinking and playing guitar all night until the right girl was writhing in his lap. In 1922 he married a woman named Roberta, and they had a son about two years later. By this time he'd gotten so fat that, when he played, the guitar would sit atop his stomach, propped beneath his chin. Mayo Williams, talent director for Paramount Records, brought Lemon to Chicago in 1925 for the first of many sessions. Although his records were a huge success, he received very little from Paramount for them. He stayed with the company probably because Williams pimped for him; at the end of a session Williams would pay the dissolute blind man with a few dollars, a bottle of booze and a prostitute. Lemon recorded over ninety sides for Paramount in three years, singing every kind of song. Never a blues specialist, by the time he began recording he'd cultivated a fluent and rather remarkable blues guitar style. He was among the most inventive lyricists in the blues genre as well. By 1930 he was the best-selling country blues singer of his time. Some of his most celebrated recordings were "Black Snake Moan," "Easy Rider Blues," "Piney Woods Money Mama," "Match Box Blues," "Jack o'Diamond Blues," "'Lectric Chair Blues" and the everlasting "See That My Grave Is Kept Clean." He recorded religious songs under the pseudonym Deacon L. J. Bates. Blind Lemon Jefferson's death is shrouded in mystery, having occurred apparently in 1930, when he froze to death on a street one night in Chicago. Ibid., p. 114. Arnold S. Caplin, *Blind Lemon Jefferson-Son House* (New York: Biograph Records, 1972), liner notes. Samuel Charters, *The Country Blues* (New York: Da Capo, 1975), pp. 57–72.

(39)

1. "That's the way I learned how to play anything I want," said Tommy Johnson long ago to his brother LeDell. Evans, op. cit., p. 23.

(40)

1. See note 36:1.

(43)

1. With the ravenous Mississippi River forever threatening the existence of life and property along its shores, flood walls known as *levees* were raised to stymie the tides. To build these levees, and to insure their efficacy with constant inspection and repair, levee *camps* were established in the backwater region between the flood walls and the river. The camps were manned by the roughest of black men, usually convicts from area prison farms, and they earned widespread notoriety for their sinister and oftentimes violent ways. On weekend nights the overworked laborers welcomed truckloads of women from the nearest towns, and they would play together until the work week began anew. Parties were held in canvas tents erected under the trees near the river, and local musicians would risk their lives to provide the entertainment.

2. The Afro-American music to be found in and around Mississippi is by no means limited to guitars, fiddles and harmonicas. In the northwest corner of the state, traditional music is performed on such instruments as panpipes (or "quills"), kazoos (or "jazz horns"), trombones, saxophones, mandolins and pianos. Most fascinating of all is the use of the fife and drum, which first came to light in 1942 when Alan Lomax recorded the Sid Hemphill band, a session of critical importance for the understanding of black music in the United States. The fife is played in combination with a bass drum and one or two snare drums, and it is made by burning holes in stalks of cane cut from a creek bottom. It is not customary for more than one fife to be played at a time, and sometimes it is used as a solo instrument. The overwhelming influence on this type of music is African. A prominent trait is the emphasis on percussion; there is even a trace of a most vital function of African percussion, the *talking drum*. David Evans, *Afro-American Folk Music from Tate and Panola Counties, Mississippi* (Washington, D.C.: Library of Congress, Music Division, AFS L67, 1978), descriptive brochure.

3. Robert Johnson was known to carry a little black book with him for several years, using it to record whatever lyrics or ideas he might hear or have in mind. He could have picked this up from his friend Ike Zinnerman.

(46)

1. Willie Brown is singing verses here from his "Future Blues" ("The minutes seem like hours, an' the hours seem like days,/ An' it seem like my woman oughtta stop her lowdown ways").

2. Son House is singing verses here from his "Jinx Blues" ("Well, the blues, the blues is a worried heart disease/ Look like the woman you be lovin', man, so doggone hard to please"), copyright 1965 by Sondick Music Company.

(48)

1. Son is singing verses from his "Preachin' the Blues Part 1" and "Preachin' the Blues Part 2." Caplin, op. cit., song lyrics.

2. According to Son House, "I Can Make My Own Songs," *Sing Out,* July 1965.

(50)

1. This may or may not have been a song performed by Robert Johnson at the time of his "debut" in Robinsonville; its title and lyrics do link it to Son House, circa 1931. This was the only one of Robert's songs to have a secondary title on file with the American Record Company, "Up Jumped the Devil." The original recording can be found on the Columbia Records LP *Robert Johnson, King of the Delta Blues Singers,* number CL 1654.

(51)

1. According to Son House, loc. cit.

(54)

1. "Cigarette Blues" was one of the many hits recorded by Bo Carter and the Mississippi Sheiks, perhaps the most popular of the 1930s Delta music groups. "The Sheiks were composed of the eleven Chatmon brothers, all of whom played a number of instruments, as their father and grandfather did before them. 'My brothers were Lonnie, Edgar, Bo, Willie, Lamar, and me,' recollected Sam Chatmon, 'plus Laurie, and Harry Chatmon, and Charlie Chatmon,' he added, forgetting to list a couple of brothers. 'I played bass viol for them, and Lonnie, he played violin and Harry, he played second violin. And my brother Bo, he played clarinet and my brother Bert played guitar and my brother Larry, he beat the drums. And my brother Harry, he played piano, you see. And my brother Bo he played guitar, too, and he even used to play tenor banjo. And I played guitar.' And as the Mississippi Sheiks they were famous from Atlanta to San Antonio, and all through the Delta. Their repertoire included country dance tunes, popular folk songs, occasional hillbilly items, blues, but their greatest success came from the many risqué songs dealing with assorted sexual mo-

tifs that they released. Although all Delta recording artists included such songs in their repertoire, no one recorded as many as the Sheiks, which helped make them highly popular with white audiences as well as black. ones. Lonnie, Sam and Harry Chatman also recorded separately, while Bo Chatman, as Bo Carter, was one of the best-known blues singers of the day." Paul Oliver, *The Story of the Blues* (London: Penguin Books, 1972), pp. 49–50.

2. Any white plantation owner was known among his tenant and itinerant laborers as the "Boss," the "bossman" or the "Big Boss," of which only the term "bossman" indicates any sort of friendly respect. The plantation system was so rigid, so solid, and the owners' authority so complete, that the blacks came to use the term "bossman" to represent oppressive white society and law in general.

(55)

1. "Get Off With Me," a vocal duet with Coot Grant (Viola B. Wilson) and Kid Wesley Wilson, accompanied by Wesley Wilson's piano, was recorded in February 1931. Sex was the one area of Afro-American life over which the ruling whites had no control. Howard "Stretch" Johnson, *Copulatin' Blues* (Tenafly, New Jersey: Stash Records, ST 101), recording notes.

2. Recipe provided by David Evans, *Tommy Johnson* (London: Studio Vista, 1971), p. 57.

(56)

1. R. D. Norwood, known as "Peg Leg Sam" or "One-Legged Sam," was born in Crystal Springs, Mississippi, in the early 1890s and was living in Jackson by 1920. He played mandolin and guitar and was regarded more highly as an accompanist than as a singer. He was one of the men Tommy Johnson played with most in the early and mid-1920s. They fought a lot too, according to the Rev. Ishmon Bracey. "A fellow we called One-Legged Sam used to play with us accompaniment. He would all the time jump on Tommy till I'd be around. He'd beat Tommy if he didn't do like he wanted him to do. He'd jump on him. He was trouble. Had one leg. He'd stand back talking with one of them crutches and before you know anything, he done knocked you down with one of 'em. He done killed two or three men with guns, knives, razors. He's just trouble. But I'm the onliest one that conquered him. Tommy wouldn't fight." Norwood moved to Chicago in 1932, where he played and recorded until his death in 1967. Ibid., p. 88.

(57)

1. "Canned Heat Blues" was Tommy Johnson's most thoroughly personal song. With the sale of liquor outlawed during Prohibition times, many men who were accustomed to drinking turned to cheaper and still legal substitutes. Sterno, called "canned heat," was one of them. How many people it killed or crippled we may never know, but these side effects of the "Great Experiment" were felt most severely by blacks, who couldn't afford to buy the more expensive bootleg liquor. There were some who drank it continually for other reasons. Mager Johnson remembers his brother developing a taste for it: "He loved that canned heat. He's the first person I ever heard tell of drinking canned heat. And he drank so much of it, he said he was going to put out a record about the canned heat. And that's where the 'Canned Heat Blues' come from. Oh, he started I don't know how many people around here in Copiah drinking that stuff. Oh shoot, I was drinking that stuff. It's a good drink." It was also a good record. The singing and guitar playing are superb, perhaps Tommy Johnson's greatest performance on disk. Ibid., pp. 57–58.

(58)

1. "Knockin' a Jug" was recorded by Louis Armstrong and His Orchestra on March 5, 1929, for Okeh Records, with Louis Armstrong on trumpet, Jack Teagarden on trombone, Happy Caldwell on tenor sax, Joe Sullivan on piano, Eddie Lang on guitar and Kaiser Marshall on drums. Frederick Ramsey, Jr., *Jazz, Vol. 7, New York: 1922–1934* (New York: Folkways Records, FJ 2807), notes.

2. Isaiah 24:1.

(60)

1. In the Southern black patois, a distinction was made between *musicianers,* characterized so by their instrumental proficiency, and *songsters,* regarded more for their singing and songwriting capabilities.

2. Black Mississippians often refer to Alabama as a Land of Death in personal conversation, storytelling and song lyrics (see Charley Patton singing "Going to Move to Alabama," Scene 93). The reverse attitude seems to be true as well. John Shines, who lived a few miles from the Mississippi border in Holt, Alabama, refused to set foot in Mississippi "because of the people"; he refused to do so for over thirty years.

3. James Hillman, *The Dream and the Underworld* (New York: Harper Colophon Books, 1979), p. 134.

4. Levees were notorious throughout the Delta for shielding not only the riverside from flood tides but "sinners" and criminals from the forces of morality as well. On the far side of the levee, in the shadows or backwater woodlands or down on the dark riverbank, every sort of character imaginable acted out his blackest fantasies in an atmosphere of sinister, oblivious dread. People gambled, drank, did drugs, made love, murdered and played their favorite music most heartfully. Pathetic attempts by the law to control such ways of the soul resulted in signs along the levees like the one depicted here.

(61)

1. Robert Johnson, seventeen years old, married Virginia Travis, fifteen years old, in Penton, Mississippi, in February 1929.

2. The recordings left by Skip James are among the greatest in country blues and establish James as one of the few bluesmen of compositional genius. A proud if not arrogant man, he looked down upon popular music recording as a tool "to deaden the mind" and "make enemies of friends," but as a practitioner he prided himself for always sounding "kinda strange to the public." He saw singing as a means to support his stylish way of living. After his discovery by H. C. Speir (see note 10:3), James left by train in early 1931 for Paramount's Wisconsin studio in the deluded belief that this recording session was a prelude to Hollywood fame. After the session, Paramount officials assured him that he would make a "terrific hit" with the twenty-six songs he recorded, inducing James to opt for deferred royalty payments as his records were issued. In 1932 he was on a breadline in Dallas, still awaiting checks for his last seven Paramount releases. When he threatened to sue, Paramount informed him of its decision to liquidate, a bitter disappointment which forced James out of the music business ("a barrel of crabs") for more than thirty years. He reverted to the part of "a plain, ordinary Skip," performing plantation labor instead of chanting other-worldly melodies, visionary laments. Ever compelled by the grandeur of success, James later characterized himself as "one of the star tractor drivers in Mississippi." Upon his strange reappearance at the 1964 Newport Folk Festival, it was evident that time had not eroded James's magnificent countertenor or his instrumental dexterity, but because of failing health he did not expect to live much longer. With almost perverse timing, the Cream rock 'n' roll band's version of his "I'm So Glad" became an international hit as he was succumbing

to cancer. His death in 1969 at the age of sixty-seven left his widow almost destitute. "Devil Got My Woman" is Skip James's masterpiece, a chilling wail of lost love from ancestral depths. "Cypress Grove Blues," "Hard Time Killing Floor Blues" and "Special Rider Blues" are other exceptional works. His recordings had a profound effect on Robert Johnson, who adapted two to his own repertoire. Stephen Calt, *Skip James, King of the Delta Blues Singers* (Canaan, N.Y.: Biograph Records BLP-12029), notes.

3. Skip James considered himself a serious musician and composer. He advanced his own musical theories and systems in addition to his songwriting and recording. Unlike most bluesmen, James called each of the standard tuning keys by their right names, save for C, which he called "C natural," but which was really E. He also used a rather definite system of string classification. From the sixth string to the first he termed them: (6) Bass, or Subtone, (5) Baritone, (4) Alto, (3 & 2) Tenors, (1) Soprano. James also refers often to triplets, 16th and 32nd and 64th notes, tonics, subdominants and 2/4 and 4/4 time, all incorrectly. It turns out that he once bought a copy of a book called *Exegesis of Musical Knowledge* from H. C. Speir's shop and looked it over a bit. Al Wilson, "Son House, An Analysis of His Music and a Biography," *Collectors Classics 14,* October 1966.

4. Jack Owens was a friend and musical associate of Skip James who has a small but commanding recording legacy of his own. He has played guitar since childhood, and is still considered the best musician around his hometown of Bentonia. He plays in the style and tone of this isolated little hilltop town, his songs, like those of James, distinctive for high melismatic singing, complex melodies, intricate guitar parts, and haunting, brooding lyrics dealing with loneliness, death and the hereafter. Altogether it is one of the eeriest, loneliest and deepest blues sounds ever recorded. Like James's "Devil Got My Woman," "It Must Have Been the Devil" is Owens' variation on an old Bentonia song theme. David Evans, *It Must Have Been the Devil, Mississippi Country Blues by Jack Owens & Bud Spires* (New York: Testament Records, T-2222), liner notes.

(69)

1. "Choose Your Seat and Set Down" exemplifies the simplicity and solemn dignity of the Afro-American spiritual. It has practical, mundane value as well, serving to usher congregants to their seats as they arrive for their church meetings. An elder of the congregation begins slowly, matching the song precisely to the tenor and tempo of the day. Congregants who already have arrived respond

with a faint chorus. The leader sings again, more strongly now. The response is stronger, and soon the spiritual will have gathered all the voices of the church into a swelling, rolling chorus. Each participant takes his own part from shrillest falsetto to deepest bass and improvises within it. These passionate songs have long comforted the Afro-American with visions of a heavenly reward. The setting and manner of the singing are strongly reminiscent of African religious practice, but the content, flowing out of the Bible and folk hymns of the whites, is distinctly Afro-American. Alan Lomax, *Afro-American Spirituals, Work Songs, and Ballads* (Washington, D.C.: The Library of Congress Music Division, AAFS L3), descriptive booklet.

2. Refer to note 37:1.

(70)

1. "Our preachers were usually plantation folks, just like the rest of us," most Delta blacks like former slave Robert Anderson would agree, except that the preacher was "called" to his office, called through some religious experience indicating to him that God had chosen him as a spiritual leader, a man who through his personal magnetism or leadership was found worthy of such a position of authority. He was expected to have some knowledge, however imperfect, of the Bible. The fact that he was acquainted with the source of sacred knowledge, which was in a sense the exclusive possession of the whites, gave him prestige in matters concerning religion and the supernatural. He had to be able to communicate his special knowledge to his people, so preaching meant dramatizing the Bible and the way of God to man. The Afro-American preachers of the South—and, later, of urban centers nationwide— were principally known for the imagery of their sermons. The "sermon" moved fluidly from speech to song to dance to moaning and back again. Once more we see the pre-eminence of the *imaginal* over the literal, of images exciting the spirit unto an ecstatic intimacy with God rather than the mere abstract sense of moral satisfaction, in the Afro-American assimilation of white reality. Rev. J. M. Gates, *I'm Going to Heaven If It Takes My Life* (New York: Riverside Records, SDP 11), discographical notes. Pete Welding, *Singing Preachers and Their Congregations* (Berkeley: America's Music Series No. 19), liner notes.

(71)

1. After an Easter Day service chanted by Sin-Killer Griffin at Darrington State Farm in Sandy Point, Texas, recorded by John A. Lomax in 1934. B. A. Botkin, *Negro Religious Songs and Services*

(Washington, D.C.: The Library of Congress, Music Division, AAFS L10), list of songs.

2. Coupled with the preacher's imaginal sermonizing was his ability to sing; the union of the two skills induced *holy dance* at one or more peaks in a service. The erotic spiritual spasms of this trance state created an image of catharsis, an image of abandonment to God, making holy dance a crucial element of the Delta form of black ecstatic worship. Welding, loc. cit.

(75)

1. Robert is singing "I'm Going to Leland," a work song of extraordinary beauty found on Library of Congress LP AAFS L3, recorded by John A. Lomax in 1936 in Parchman, Mississippi. "I went to Leland, Lord, I thought I was lost. . . ."

(78)

1. When Virginia became pregnant in the summer of 1929, Robert became a proud expectant father who now considered himself to be a farmer more than a musician. His dreams for his wife and family were suddenly destroyed when both Virginia and the baby died in childbirth, in April 1930.

(79)

1. "God Don't Never Change" was recorded by Blind Willie Johnson (see note 2:2) in New Orleans on December 10, 1929.

2. The Yazoo River (Choctaw for "River of Death") starts near Greenwood, runs parallel with U.S. Highway 61 to Redwood, where it diverges and ceases its flow just north of Vicksburg.

(82)

1. In certain isolated spots around the Delta one may still find vestiges of the earliest type of Afro-American religious song, the *ring shout*. True to an ancient West African practice, the dancers shuffle round and round in single file, clapping out the beat in complex counterrhythms. Once an integral part of serious religious observance before its gradual disappearance from the church service or holiness meeting, Delta communities started to reintroduce the ring shout as a means to secure for the Church young people wanting to dance. It soon became permissible for the community to gather in the church on Saturday nights to watch couples promenade around the outside aisle. Alan Lomax, *Afro-American Spirituals, Work Songs, and Ballads,* descriptive booklet.

2. For Calletta Craft, see note 118:1.

(89)

1. According to historian and folklorist Mack McCormick, a striking and very strange characteristic of Robert Johnson was his regular tendency towards sudden changes in appearance and outlook, oftentimes accompanied by alterations of name and behavior. This made biographical research difficult later on, as few people living today could be sure that it was really Robert Johnson who had crossed their path so long ago.

(91)

1. Neumann, op. cit., p. 166.

(93)

1. When Charley Patton documented external events in song, such events were inevitably local ones. "Moon Going Down," one of the fastest pieces in his repertoire, mentions the fiery climax to the Clarksdale cotton mill's demise. By associating this with personal rejection in love, the outward suggestion of incoherence in Patton's songwriting bows to the greater suggestion of alchemical genius, as his images link through rhythm and melody as elements of hallucination. Full of rough human energy, crude and fine and abusive of every rule, this song belongs to the "descending bass" category even though its bass notes have been replaced by thumping or banging sounds. This would be done by hitting the guitar with the right hand and was what Son House referred to as Patton's "clowning." Perls, Calt, et al., loc. cit.

2. George "Bullet" Williams was a recording artist from Selma, Alabama, who was skillful on harmonica. Like many country harmonica players, Williams eschewed melodic concerns for imaginal ones in his recordings, using his harmonica to mock trains ("Frisco Leaving Birmingham") and mimic nature ("The Escaped Convict"). Oliver, op. cit., pp. 48–49.

3. "Going to Move to Alabama" was Charley Patton's "cover" of one of the biggest hits of the era, Jim Jackson's "Kansas City Blues." The guitar-vocal interplay is brilliant here, the lyrics bizarre ("I got up this mornin' my hat in my hand./ Didn't have no woman or have no man./ I done been to Alabama, graveyard to be her home"). See note 60:2.

---

(94)

1. Sometime after his twentieth birthday, friends of Robert Johnson remember seeing a "white spot" growing in over part of his left eye. This "spot," which stayed with Robert until the end of his life, was probably a *pterygium* (from the Greek *pteryx*, meaning "wing" or "winglike"), an abnormal mass of mucous membrane growing over the cornea. This affliction is not uncommon among people who spend much of their time outdoors.

2. While they were living for a spell in Cleveland, Mississippi, Bertha Lee had a fight with Charley and cut his throat with a butcher's knife. She would never, of course, discuss the matter, but the story is well known around Cleveland. That Patton survived, with a scar on his throat, and stayed with Bertha Lee is well established. Fahey, op. cit., p. 25.

(95)

1. "Stone Pony Blues" was a 1934 remake of Charley Patton's great "Pony Blues" in a different key. Although this number lacked nothing in clarity or precision, the extraordinary relaxed quality of "Pony Blues" seems to degenerate in performance here into laziness or sheer fatigue or an extension of his bodily state. Perls, Calt, et al., loc. cit.

2. This mythical duel between Robert Johnson and Charley Patton, a ritual commonly practiced among Afro-American musicians as *headhunting* or *headcutting*, is contested with verses from different Charley Patton songs. After Charley opens with three verses from "Stone Pony Blues," Robert challenges him with a stanza from "Pony Blues"; Charley reverts to "Stone Pony" again and is matched by Robert, singing almost the same verse; Charley jumps to "Rattlesnake Blues," Robert picks up the last line Charley sings and rhymes it with a line elsewhere in the song, then Charley struggles through the last verse of "Rattlesnake" to the final word, before conceding defeat.

(96)

1. "Walkin' Blues," a seductive boogie with a downbeat that still astonishes, is a popular Robert Johnson song often recorded by blues and rock musicians over the last forty years. A 1942 recording of it by Son House and band at Clack's Store in Lake Cormorant, Mississippi, released on the British Flyright label ("Walking Blues," FLY 541), is a remarkable document of the song as it might have sounded on the street or in the jook.

2. In this scene, young John Shines is spotted by Robert concentrating hard on the performer's musical technique. Competition being what it was, and Robert being ever so self-protective in his enigmatic alienation, he would frequently flee in the middle of a performance if he felt in the least bit paranoid. Both John Shines and David "Honeyboy" Edwards (see Scene 228) have recalled incidents long ago when they would commence performing with Robert Johnson, only to discover a while later that he had slipped away unnoticed, and often they wouldn't see him again for days or weeks, if at all.

(97)

1. In 1933, Charley Patton and Bertha Lee moved to Holly Ridge, where they often performed together locally. Patton was suffering greatly at this time from both his damaged throat and a heart ailment, probably a mitral valve condition, of which he was soon to die. He was chronically out of breath, and it would take him two or three days to recuperate from a night's singing. Fahey, loc. cit.

(100)

1. Friars Point was a town much frequented by itinerant black musicians in the thirties, and Hirsberg's Drugstore there was a favorite gathering place for musician and audience. The proprietor of the store, which is still owned and operated by the Hirsberg family, regularly paid musicians to display their wares outside the store in order to attract customers. This was a commonplace practice throughout the South.

2. Another popular Robert Johnson number, "Sweet Home Chicago" offers a refrain of such peculiar geographical logic as to cause much confused debate among those familiar with the song. The lyrics in question suggest that the singer is asking a girlfriend if she wants to go to "the land of California, my sweet home, Chicago," a place that to most people does not exist. Some people say the reference is to a specific California-to-Illinois train route; the author found this difficult to apply to Delta reality, preferring to think of the refrain as a reference to something of the spirit, of the psyche, a train route of the mind. Recently, however, historian Mack McCormick claimed that Robert had a cousin living in the tiny California town of Port of Chicago. "Sweet Home Chicago" is available on the Columbia LP *Robert Johnson, King of the Delta Blues Singers, Vol. II,* number C 30034.

227

(101)

1. "Ramblin' on My Mind" is sung by Robert in slightly different versions on the Columbia *Robert Johnson, King of the Delta Blues* albums (CL 1654 and C 30034), and on the limited edition Roots LP *Delta Blues* (RL-339), produced in Austria.

2. Friars Point old-timer Lonnie Bass recalls such an incident occurring during a Charley Patton street performance fifty years ago. Robert was known to draw similarly large and unrestrained crowds as well.

(104)

1. "Travelin' Riverside Blues," found on the first Columbia *Robert Johnson* LP, strangely became an international white adolescent anthem in 1969 when the British rock group Led Zeppelin appropriated certain lyrics for the hit song "Whole Lotta Lovin'."

2. Another image from the memory of Lonnie Bass, corroborated by David Evans (*Tommy Johnson*).

(105)

1. Field hollering was a common form of communication, chant and catharsis among Afro-American field workers in the South. Many outstanding blues songs stem directly from these hollers, which in turn are West African in origin. Son House recorded a holler for the Library of Congress in 1941 (AFS L59). Other hollers, also called *arhoolies*, have been included in the Folkways LP *Negro Folk Music of Alabama*, recorded by Harold Courlander (FE 4417).

(106)

1. At least one Jackson record shop actually advertised its stock to black laborers this way, and a flier such as this one did in fact exploit the death of Charley Patton for personal gain. Oliver, op. cit., pp. 106–24.

(108)

1. Charley Patton once made his home in Lula, Mississippi, and wrote a song called "Dry Well Blues" which documented a terrible drought there ("Lord, you oughta been there, Lord,/ These womens all leave this town . . .").

2. "The Devil's Dream" is a unique aural vision not unlike nightmare played on ten-note quills, accompanied by snare and bass

drums, with vocal effects by Sid Hemphill (see note 43:2). Although there is a well-known British-American fiddle tune called "The Devil's Dream," this performance seems to be but distantly related to its other strain. The fiddle tune here has been transformed into an entirely different instrumental piece. The quills used are panpipes which have been replaced today by the harmonica. Panpipe technique found in "The Devil's Dream" is African in nature, where alternating blown and whooped notes is very common. Images created are dark and discordant, but members of Delta communities are never heard remarking that the music is weird or out of tune. Evans, *Afro-American Folk Music from Tate and Panola Counties, Mississippi*, descriptive brochure.

3. A real person documented in history (see note 71:1), and myth.

(109)

1. After a sermon delivered by the Rev. F. McGhee in 1930, and found today on America's Music Series *Singing Preachers* collection BC 19, edited by Chris Strachwitz.

2. Released just two months before his death, Charley Patton's "Poor Me" is the only one of his thirty-odd recordings that could be termed "sentimental." Despite the song's melodic beauty, the performance is basically a tired one and lacks the power and rhythmic control of the early Patton. Perls, Calt, et al., loc. cit.

(110)

1. "Jesus Is My Air-O-Plane" was recorded in Chicago in 1930 by Mother McCollum, about whom no information is available. Gayle Dean Wardlow, *In the Spirit, Vol. 2* (Berkeley: Origin Jazz Library, OJL-13), notes.

(113)

1. "If I Had Possession of Judgment Day" is a powerful blues on the traditional "Rollin' and Tumblin'" theme. Robert's version begins with an unusual religious commentary in the first verse, then follows it with verses also used by Hambone Willie Newbern and Son House. Found on Columbia LP CL 1654.

2. Sin-Killer Griffin's "sermon" here is one that dates back to slavery days and is taken in this instance from a spontaneous sermon rendered by Charley Patton during his recording of "You're Gonna Need Somebody When You Die." The imagery is derived from Revelations.

3. This chant was taken from a field recording made by David and Cheryl Evans entitled "Old Dick Jones Is Dead and Gone," performed by Compton Jones and family with "bow diddley" (or "one-string"—see note 16:1), chair, cans and benches. Issued by the Library of Congress on album AFS L67.

(114)

1. Houston Stackhouse reports the story, however apocryphal, that once Robert took an audience away from a singing evangelist by confronting him directly and publicly. If this did, in fact, take place, it would have been a highly unusual occurrence in the timid black Baptist Delta.

(115)

1. "After the Ball Is Over" is an old fife and drum piece taken from the waltz "After the Ball," which was composed by Charles K. Harris in 1892 and is still popular with country string bands today. The present version was performed by the Sid Hemphill Band on fife, two snare drums and a bass drum, and was recorded for the Library of Congress (AFS L67) by Alan Lomax in 1942.

2. Robert Johnson was known to favor a big Gibson guitar in public performance, using another guitar, a Kalamazoo, for special occasions.

(118)

1. Robert Johnson married Calletta Craft at the Copiah County courthouse in May 1931. She was a generous, affectionate woman ten years Robert's senior who had been married twice before and had three small children.

(119)

1. Robert reportedly insisted that his marriage to Calletta be kept a strict secret.

(121)

1. The *ring game* was once a familiar sight among both white and black children in the South. The game was both European and African, with English rhymes and melodies and African rhythms and punctuation. The "Satisfied" theme was a common one. Sometimes the word "satisfied" related meaningfully to the lyrics, other times it related to the rhythm. Courlander, *Negro Folk Music of Alabama,* notes.

(126)

1. John Shines remembered working as a herdsman, tending cows by the riverside, sleeping nights beneath the hood of a car. "The river was full of song," Shines said, "many of it the same as in the fields."

2. "Come On in My Kitchen" is a truly haunting mating call in Spanish tuning, a song in which Robert Johnson's bottleneck guitar follows the vocal line perfectly as it assumes the timbre of the human voice itself. John Shines reported that this song made men and women cry when Robert would play it for them. Found on Columbia CL 1654 and on Roots RL-339, in different takes.

(128)

1. All of the great Afro-American musicians of the day came through West Helena, Arkansas, a town just across the Mississippi River from Friars Point. Popular with Mississippians who liked to cross the river for a legal drink, a ferry could be taken for a dime or a skiff for a nickel. Robert Nighthawk, Roosevelt Sykes and Hacksaw Harney (see Scene 145) were among the many exceptional musicians who gravitated to West Helena.

2. The *Katy Adams* did, in fact, exist, transporting prostitutes who would entice clientele by jiggling coins in the manner described.

(129)

1. Calvin Frazier, who recorded for the Library of Congress in 1938.

(130)

1. William Ferris, *Blues from the Delta* (Garden City, N.Y.: Anchor Press/Doubleday, 1978), photograph.

2. A singer with a recording career almost as prodigious as Lonnie Johnson's, Tampa Red was dubbed "The Guitar Wizard" for his deft playing of the slide guitar (see note 3:4). He was born Hudson Whittaker in Atlanta on Christmas Day, 1900, and spent most of his childhood in Tampa, Florida. In the mid-twenties he went to Chicago, where a short stint with Ma Rainey proved to be his breakthrough. It was here that he also met Tom Dorsey, who came to be known as Georgia Tom (see Scene 131). Tampa Red stopped the religious Tom from joining the Church by having him set a song he'd written to music. The number turned out to be "It's

Tight Like That," and became the first in a series of bawdy commercial hits for the duo. Recognizing a new market in the Southern
blacks now living in urban areas who turned away from immediate
anxiety for fond remembrances of rural life, Tampa Red formed his
Hokum Jug Band, also known as The Hokum Boys. The group was
extremely successful and came to be copied by several other
"hokum" bands, all of them specializing similarly in good, dirty
fun. Tampa Red continued to perform with new bands such as his
Chicago Five, dazzling all with his rich, ringing guitar and, unlike
Robert Johnson (who had a chordal approach), single-string melodic runs. He recorded into the 1950s, his work being available
today principally on the RCA-Bluebird and Yazoo labels. Oliver,
op. cit., pp. 100–1.

(131)

1. Frankie "Half-Pint" Jaxon was something of an anomaly in the
world of Afro-American music. Although he was born in Mont-
gomery, Alabama, in 1895, he was raised in Kansas City, where his
shrill feminine voice stood apart from the local sound. He worked
his way through the South and made a hit in Atlantic City as a female impersonator, then sang with King Oliver in Chicago at the
Sunset Café and the Plantation. In the late twenties Jaxon hooked
up with Tampa Red, touring and recording with the Hokum Jug
Band. His superior female vocal technique and brilliant sense of
timing contributed to making "It's Tight Like That," "She Loves
So Good" and his mockery of Leroy Carr's "How Long How Long
Blues" ribald classics. He later sang with Cow Cow Davenport and
the Harlem Hamfats, moving from jazz band to vaudeville to
hokum Chicago folk blues with considerable ease. Ibid., pp. 67–69.

2. Thomas A. "Georgia Tom" Dorsey was born in Villa Rica,
Georgia, in 1899, and learned to play piano by listening to the
likes of Lark Lee, Soap Stick and Long Boy perform in clubs
around Atlanta. After failing miserably as a steelworker in Gary,
Indiana, Dorsey organized a band for Ma Rainey in Chicago, playing piano for her from that point on for several years. He met
Tampa Red at Ma's last recording session in 1928 and worked with
Tampa to introduce a suave, wry, yet saucy form of urban blues.
In 1932, Dorsey's young wife Nettie died in childbirth while he
was on the road. The sorrow-stricken man rushed home to bury
her, finding comfort there in his newborn baby girl. Then the baby
died also. Dorsey quit blues and jazz altogether, became an or-
dained Baptist minister, and sang the gospel for over fifty years
before his death in 1992. "Precious Lord," a gospel hymn he wrote
immediately following his wife's death, is one of the most beautiful

spirituals ever composed. Bob Rusch, "Georgia Tom Dorsey—Interview," *Cadence, The American Review of Jazz and Blues,* December 1978. Oliver, loc. cit.

(132)

1. According to bluesman Houston Stackhouse, several eminent Delta musicians had formal arrangements with agents for representation.

2. Hacksaw Harney was one of the finest guitarists of his day. See note 128:1.

(134)

1. "How Long How Long Blues" was a best-selling song of the early thirties, and helped establish Frankie Jaxon as a vocal humorist without equal until Fats Waller emerged a few years later. In this performance, Jaxon takes the "how long" refrain from an existing blues standard and reduces it through insane repetition to utter absurdity. The lewd transformation of the literal image is obvious. Found on an LP entitled *Party Blues,* Melodeon Records (MLP 7324).

(137)

1. In 1936, Jackson music shop owner H. C. Speir (see note 10:3), disillusioned by now with the record business and reducing his direct involvement with it, sent word nevertheless to another informal talent scout working in the area, Ernie Oertle, about an impressive young guitar player named Robert Johnson. Oertle was the American Record Company's salesman for the Mid-South in the late 1930s and would audition musicians whose paths crossed his on his route. After receiving Robert Johnson's name and address from Speir, Oertle sought out the prospect for an audition in the fall of 1936.

2. "Walter 'Buddy Boy' Hawkins was probably born between 1885 and 1900 in Blytheville, Arkansas, where it seems he spent most of his life; anything else about the man must be inferred from his music, recorded in 1927 and 1929. Because his music is unique and apparently without precedent in the blues idiom, it is precisely in his music that inference becomes difficult. Hawkins used the blues format merely as a framework into which he put contents that might have astonished his contemporaries. His music relied on a harmonic structure far richer than the typical blues piece, with incomparable guitar accompaniments that were *contrapuntally* conceived, usually in four voices. Also, several of his recorded

songs betray an unmistakable influence of classical flamenco techniques; one can only speculate where Hawkins came in contact with this music. One guess is that he served in Europe during World War I, as did Son House. Europe had no discernible effect on House's music, but Hawkins may have been more impressionable. Then again, he might have picked it up in New Orleans." According to his introductory jive spoken at the outset of two recordings, Hawkins hailed from Jackson and Birmingham as well as Blytheville. He disappeared without a trace a few years after making his records, and it is doubtful that he is alive today. Jerome Epstein, *Buddy Boy Hawkins and His Buddies* (New York: Yazoo Records, L-1010), liner notes.

(138)

1. "I Believe I'll Dust My Broom" is Robert Johnson's most famous song in the latter-day blues universe, but this is due mainly to the hit record by Elmore James recorded fourteen years later. It is a dance tune that, in Robert's version, powers vigorously to a surging peak in the last two verses. The song was influenced by Leroy Carr's "I Believe I'll Make a Change" and Kokomo Arnold's "Sissy Man Blues," among others. The phrase "dust my broom" here is an idiomatic expression which means "to leave town." Found on Columbia C 30034.

(139)

1. The rise to power of Emperor Haile Selassie and his Ethiopian empire's invasion by Italy in 1935 created a great deal of interest among Afro-Americans. John Shines told the author that he and Robert discussed Ethiopia on several occasions, with Robert reportedly concerning himself in particular with the place of Ethiopia within a biblical context.

(141)

1. Actually, Oertle drove Robert to San Antonio himself.

2. Don Law represented the American Record Company's Dallas and San Antonio operations back in the 1930s. As head of Columbia Records' Country and Western Division he produced and recorded Bob Wills and Johnny Cash, who called Law his greatest influence as a professional musician.

(143)

1. Robert deserted Calletta, who suffered a severe breakdown and

called for her family in Hazlehurst to retrieve her. She died a few years later without ever seeing Robert again.

(144)

1. Southern Afro-American vendors wandering the streets would announce their presence with a rhythmic chant, a semimusical expression that sometimes achieved a haunting, other-worldly, innocent beauty. Two examples of such chanting are to be found on the Riverside LP *A History of Classic Jazz* (SDP 11), the recordings having been made on the streets of Charleston, South Carolina, in the early part of this century.

(148)

1. "'Ragtime Texas' Henry Thomas was a singular and important figure in American musical and cultural history. Born in the bottomlands of the Sabine River in East Texas, probably in the mid-to late 1880s, Thomas grew to be a hobo, a vagabond, a big hulking black man whose charismatic singing earned him legendary renown along the Texas & Pacific Railroad line and elsewhere. People still like to remember a time when he came to 'help out' once at a country dance long ago, or they smile to recapture the image of him singing on a sunny street corner somewhere. He walked through hundreds of cities and towns, his clothes and guitar slung onto his back, a soldier in the army of homeless men drifting about the country as they pleased. His musical and cultural heritage was from the final generation of slaves, a major reason why his twenty-three recordings are among the most significant in American musical history. It's good-time music reaching out from another age: reels, anthems, stomps, gospel songs, dance calls, ballads, blues and folk fragments, giving us a blurred glimpse of Afro-American music as it existed in the last century. Thomas' guitar playing was rudimentary, executed with a thrusting drive that evokes a country dance. He used one of the most ancient of all instruments, the panpipe (or "quills"), to punch out melodies or create natural images. These songs shed a new wisp of half-light on a long lingering mystery: the origin of the blues. He provides varied examples of the idiom at several early stages of development, returning frequently to its most archaic forms. The recordings continually underscore the everlasting irony that so much of America's most expressive and vital poetry has been composed by an illiterate, uneducated people." Among the finest Ragtime Texas recordings are "Red River Blues," "Honey, Won't You Allow Me One More Chance?" "Woodhouse Blues," "Shanty Blues," "Railroadin' Some" and "Don't Leave Me Here," his final effort. Henry Thomas drifted

from view after his 1929 recording sessions, his existence confirmed just one more time—if it really was Thomas on the corner of Crawford and Capitol in Houston during the winter of 1949. The Ragtime Texas legacy has been brilliantly collected and edited, with extensive notes and song annotation, in record and text form. Mack McCormick, *Henry Thomas, "Ragtime Taxas"* (Glen Cove, N.Y.: Herwin Records, Herwin 209), biographical notes.

2. "Jonah in the Wilderness" is a narrative gospel song recorded by Henry Thomas in 1927. This is a version of the biblical tale in which Jonah, seen as a reluctant prophet, is not unlike a typical unfaithful or backsliding Christian. One must be familiar with the Book of Jonah to understand this difficult song, while recognizing that, in folk religion, Christian symbols mix fluidly with Old Testament tales. Henry Thomas has chosen to omit the best-known part of the story here, the part in which a "great fish" swallows Jonah and three days later vomits him out onto dry land. Ibid., song annotation.

(149)

1. Directly related in spirit to the black chanting vendors (see note 144:1), black train callers created strangely beautiful aural images with their periodic, unamplified announcements at the train depots. A good example of such a train caller was documented for the Library of Congress in 1936 by John A. Lomax (available on AFS L61).

(152)

1. During the latter half of the nineteenth century, southeastern Texas experienced a small but concentrated wave of German immigration that settled in the San Antonio-Austin-Houston triangle. Primarily a farming people, the Germans introduced a new language and cultural sense to the area's inhabitants, some of whom were Afro-Americans. Many black people were eventually hired by the new immigrants for farm and domestic labor, and to this day one can find traces of the linguistic and cultural influence that the Germans had on them. "Ragtime Texas" Henry Thomas was one of scores of itinerant minstrels hailing from the region who were capable of singing in German—sometimes French as well—in addition to English.

2. This silly snippet of barroom dialog between the two black cowboys and the white cowboy is translated as follows:

> BC 1: "Where would you say most people die?"
> WC: "In bed, naturally."

> BC 2: "Then how can someone ever go to bed at night with-
> out being terrified!"
> WC: "Whoa! Partner!"

(155)

1. From *The Blues According to Lightnin' Hopkins,* an essential documentary film by Les Blank.

(156)

1. This recording of "Stormy Weather" is taken from a 1933 Hollywood movie short entitled *Bundle of Blues,* made by Paramount Pictures. The vocalist in Duke Ellington's 1933 band here was Miss Ivie Anderson, who was temporarily replaced a year later by Billie Holiday. The LP on which this recording can be found is a limited edition for the Swedish Duke Ellington Society, *Duke Ellington in Hollywood/ On the Air, 1933–40,* Max Records (MLP-1001).

(160)

1. "Kindhearted Woman Blues" is an innocently emotive slow blues that, despite its deceptively simple nature, is without compare in the Robert Johnson repertoire. His sudden shift to falsetto voice in the interlude, coupled with several delicate guitar touches of extreme complexity throughout, is remarkable. Found on Columbia LPs CL 1654 and C 30034, in different takes.

(161)

1. According to the daily schedule sheets for the ARC studios in the Gunter Hotel, Adolph and the Bohemians was one of the bands set for rehearsal and recording time along with Robert Johnson's solo "act." The group was one of the many ensembles headed by regional musical stalwart Adolph Hofner, who often worked in tandem with his brother Emil. Hofner became one of the biggest names in western swing and was featured on radio station KTSA in San Antonio. Richard Stephan Aldrich, *Western Swing, Vol. 2* (Berkeley: Arhoolie Records, Old Timey LP 116), liner notes. Access to the studio schedule sheets provided by Mack McCormick.

2. Robert was to record twenty-nine original songs, and he had numerous others in store and in various stages of development. The record company racial divisions were only interested in an artist's original material, which resulted in a kaleidoscopic array of black popular songs blending in and out of one another through

veils of camouflage. Robert's ".32-20 Blues" (see Scene 174), for example, stands apart from antecedents ".20-20 Blues" by Skip James and Roosevelt Sykes's ".44 Blues," which were recorded years earlier.

3. Robert was born to Julia Dodds and her lover Noah Johnson in Hazlehurst, Mississippi, and spent the first two years of his life in Delta migrant worker camps with his mother. Julia reunited with her husband, Charlie Spencer, in 1914, and with Robert she went to Memphis to live with Spencer, as his wife and child. When she left Robert and his baby sister Carrie to make it on her own, the young boy faced two more years living with the Spencers before he was able to return to his mother once again in Robinsonville. See notes 1:4 and 4:6.

(162)

1. The use of liquor by record companies to heighten the effectiveness of its black recording artists is well known, but its well-regulated place in the proceedings did nothing to hamper their orderly, productive character. In his research, the author found only one instance wherein a singer was "likkered up" so much he could not record, the singer in this case being, not unexpectedly, Tommy Johnson (see note 4:3).

(164)

1. Recording engineers attending to country blues sessions often concerned themselves with the percussive effects of the feet in a recording. When such sounds were unwanted, pillows were placed underneath the performer's feet as indicated here; if foot-stomping was seen as an aid to the rhythm of a piece, then an extra microphone was deployed near the floor.

(165)

1. This incident in the ARC studio reported by Don Law.

2. Andres Berlanga and Francisco Montalvo were renowned musicians as solo artists who collaborated on some of the finest recordings in the annals of Texas-Mexican music. They were listed on the same recording schedule as Robert Johnson.

3. The song being sung here is "El Deportado (The Deportee)," a *corrido* popularized on record by Los Hermanos Banuelos and by Luna & Gallegos around 1930. A corrido is a ballad of the Mexican and Mexican-American oral tradition that keeps alive heroes and important events for generation after generation. The word *corrido*

means "to run" or "to flow," suggesting that these songs are running stories, or narrative ballads, usually colored by the amount of information which the corrido maker has at hand. Essential to the message and effect of a corrido is its emotional content, as is evident in "El Deportado," a song bemoaning the plight of a naive Mexican immigrant in his new home. A powerful musical and cultural tradition—and a source of historical detail—the corrido is in a state of decay today after flourishing for over one hundred years. Folklyric Records 9004. *Corridos, Part 1: 1930–1934* (Hermanos Bañuelos, Pedro Rocha & Lupe Martinez, Nacho & Justino, Hermanos Sanchez & Linares), edited by Chris Strachwitz.

(166)

1. "When You Got a Good Friend" is a Robert Johnson song recorded with the same guitar accompaniment as "Sweet Home Chicago" (see note 100:2). This unusual thirteen-bar blues remained unissued and unknown until 1961, when it was released on Columbia CL 1654.

(168)

1. "Cross Road Blues" is Robert Johnson's psychodramatic twist to the traditional "traveling blues" theme, a stark and powerful fourteen-bar blues with profoundly evocative imagery. Here we find the innocent singer lost at a backwoods crossroads at sundown, feeling isolated and frightened by the descending darkness. With this work we begin to see Robert's songs emerging as testimony not only to the earthly reality witnessed by the young black songwriter but to his inner psychic landscape as well, by means of the very same words. He performs the song with feverish emotion, biting his images through clenched teeth, growling with spare breath, barely maintaining vocal control. It is the one Robert Johnson song that mentions a real acquaintance of his by name, this person being Robert's "friendboy" Willie Brown (see note 3:2). Many singers have recorded versions of this great song, the most popular rendition having been made by Eric Clapton with his band Cream, a rendition that also includes a verse from Robert's "Traveling' Riverside Blues" (see note 104:2). Found on Columbia CL 1654 and Roots RL-339.

(169)

1. By 1936 it still could not be assumed that every singer had direct familiarity with a microphone prior to recording, particularly those who lived in such primitive realms as the Afro-American

Delta. By listening carefully to Robert Johnson's recordings, one can discern a tendency of his to turn his head away from the microphone in moments of intense emotion, thereby diminishing the impression of the voice on parts of the recording.

(171)

1. Robert Johnson's first issued record featured "Terraplane Blues," a spectacle of guitar and vocal technique and the piece for which he is best remembered in the Delta today. An extraordinary amount of careful preparation went into the creation of this work as is evident by the one-string slide, the rhythmic damping of the strings, the startling shifts to falsetto, and the tight ironic lyrics so well suited for the melody. Upon its release in 1937, "Terraplane Blues" caught the imagination of the Delta community, affecting it rather profoundly. And the unabashed autoeroticism of this driving song's wordplay still makes Buddy McCoy and the boys in Friars Point double over with laughter. Found on Columbia CL 1654.

(173)

1. ".32-20 Blues" is Robert Johnson's fastest recorded song and a direct copy of Skip James's ".22-20 Blues," which was a copy itself of Roosevelt Sykes's ".44 Blues." Robert took all of James's verses and tried to change location references, but in the recording he forgetfully mentions Wisconsin, where James recorded, rather than somewhere in his aforementioned Hot Springs, Arkansas. Nevertheless, the imagery of the lyrics ("Man, I just can't get my rest/ With this .32-20 layin' up an' down my breast") coheres well with other Robert Johnson songs, aided by three original verses added by Robert because his fast tempo made the old version by itself too brief to record. Found on Columbia CL 1654.

(175)

1. "They're Red Hot" is Robert Johnson's sole "hokum" piece (see note 130:2) and comic performance number. His sense of humor here seems largely derivative, but his arrangement and delivery of the lyrics are quite exciting to hear. No matter how he may try to mask it, however, something dark is lurking inside this token ditty. Found on Columbia C 30034.

(176)

1. "Dead Shrimp Blues" is a modest Robert Johnson recording featuring dead shrimp as a peculiar sexual image. Found on Columbia C 30034.

240

(177)

1. "Last Fair Deal Gone Down" is a highly rhythmic eight-bar blues bearing distinct elements first found in works by Blind Lemon Jefferson (see note 37:1) and "Ragtime Texas" Henry Thomas (see note 148:1). The primitive, repetitive chanting of the refrain betrays its antiquated roots, as does its subject matter, which places the song's origin in southern Mississippi migrant labor camps. Robert probably first heard the original inspiration for his "Last Fair Deal Gone Down" from his Hazlehurst mentor Ike Zinnerman (see note 22:2). Robert's spontaneous evocation of church bells in the last verse is a lovely surprise. Found on Columbia CL 1654.

(186)

1. When looking for work during the bad times of the Great Depression, musicians in San Antonio would put their talent up for grabs in front of the Ayala Drugstore on Laredo Street. Most groups or lone performers, blues singers to Texas yodelers to *corridistas* (see note 165:3), were to be had for twenty-five cents per hour or ten cents a song. Sonnichsen, loc. cit.

2. "98 Degree Blues," a field-holler song recorded in the 1920s by Alger "Texas" Alexander, a popular singer directly related to the great contemporary bluesman Lightnin' Hopkins. Eric Sackheim, *The Blues Line, A Collection of Blues Lyrics* (New York: Schirmer Books, 1975), p. 122.

(187)

1. Andres Berlanga (see note 165:2) was among many people who kiddingly referred to the San Antonio produce area as "Manure Plaza." See note 165:3.

(188)

1. "Down on Me" is a traditional Afro-American spiritual recorded by John A. and Ruby T. Lomax for the Library of Congress in 1940. Sung by Dock Reed of Livingston, Alabama, this solemn and very moving version was the basis for an aggressively less reverential recording by Texan Janis Joplin almost thirty years later. Found on AAFS L10, the Library of Congress LP *Negro Religious Songs and Services*.

(191)

1. This is a vague and utterly apocryphal account of one of Robert

Johnson's romances. David "Honeyboy" Edwards was privy to the tryst as it really was: "I had a cousin, Willie Mae Cross, and he [Robert] used to go see her and that was her boyfriend. That's how I got 'quainted with him a lot, too. And she stayed at Tunica, towards Lula, and he lived at Robinsonville, so when he was in the country playing guitar—he was a country boy just like all of us—he used to come over her house and visit her, 'cause she was his girl-friend. Then he started traveling around through the country play-ing for country dances like I was and, fact of the business, some of these guys picked him up and he recorded. That's when he got popular, you know. I don't know how he got a chance to record for this guy, I don't know how he got in touch with him, but he got in touch with him somehow." Pete Welding, "David 'Honeyboy' Ed-wards," *Blues Unlimited 54,* June 1968. See note 228:1. As for the characterization of the woman, the image here was derived not from any description of Willie Mae Cross herself but from John Shines's account given to the author of Robert's predilection for older, physically unattractive women as he himself got older.

(193)

1. See note 144:1.

(194)

1. Charles R. Townsend, *San Antonio Rose—The Life and Music of Bob Wills* (Urbana, Ill.: University of Illinois Press, 1976), p. 116.

2. The "Light Crust Doughboys" Texas swing band recorded on the same days as Robert Johnson did in June 1937, as the ARC schedule sheets indicate. W. Lee "Pappy" O'Daniel, originally a salesman for Burris Mills and later a governor of Texas, was re-sponsible for hiring the original Light Crust Doughboys—Bob Wills, Herman Arnspiger, Milton Brown—to advertise flour on the radio. When Wills and Brown left the band, O'Daniel reorganized and stepped in as master of ceremonies. The third incarnation of the Doughboys emerged under the direction of Cecil Brower in 1937. Aldrich, loc. cit. Ray Doggett, *Light Crust Doughboys, Vol. 1* (Houston: Aolt Records, Aolt 101), liner notes.

(196)

1. "Stones in My Passway" confronts and then confesses to a nightmarish corner of reality occupied by young Robert Johnson, with imagery howling from another world. It reflects the singer in his most delicate, most precious and direct musical state, as he so

desperately documents the grim condition of his soul. The recording is dead serious, the plea is real, his confessional candor stark and slightly unnerving. Robert performs the song with an uncomplicated, almost timid guitar accompaniment, his innocent voice guiding the way towards the emotional climax, "Plea-hease! Let us be friends!" that eases a sort of biblical suffering. Found on Columbia CL 1654.

(200)

1. At this point in his life, according to both Mack McCormick and John Shines, Robert began to manifest an urgent, almost obsessive need to meet his natural father, Noah Johnson. See note 4:6.

2. After recording the first of what normally would have been two or three takes to "Honeymoon Blues," Robert was instructed by Don Law to prepare for a second take. Robert's reply, "I want to go with our next one, myself," was etched into the original master recording of the next song and is our only spoken-word document of Robert Johnson. As it turned out, the song that prompted the unusual remark was "Love in Vain."

3. "Love in Vain" is Robert Johnson at his most innocent. The song's character is striking: it is a blues ballad, a love song and lament at once, set to a melody that was floating around the Jackson area in the early 1930s. The origin of the song is ages old, and Ike Zinnerman may have been the one who taught Robert the third verse to "Love in Vain," which also appeared eleven years before in Blind Lemon Jefferson's first record, "Dry Southern Blues." This is Robert Johnson's most celebrated song today, principally because of the worldwide impact of the Rolling Stones' renditions of "Love in Vain" on their "Let It Bleed" and "Get Your Ya-Yas Out!" LPs. Found on Columbia C 30034, with a second take available on Roots RL-339 and Historical HLP-31.

(206)

1. "Me and the Devil Blues" is a slow, sinister, uncannily dramatic song, a surreal vision of some poor soul waking into the good side of Damnation, a born-again satanic pact confessed. The spiritual commitment that pronounced itself first in "Crossroad Blues" and "Stones in My Passway" proceeds in mythic ceremony here. Robert proclaims communion with an "ol' evil spirit," then arrogantly tells one and all where to bury his dead body. See note 243:3. Found on Columbia CL 1654.

(208)

1. According to Mack McCormick and bluesman Lee Jackson, who claimed that he was a companion of Robert's during his last recording sessions, Robert traveled throughout southern Texas and played a few Mexican jooks below the border as well.

(210)

1. "Hellhound on My Trail" is unique in Afro-American music not for considerations of structure, or melody, or style, but for the riveting vividness of its aural imagery. Hailing from a desolate world in which sex is the only salvation, Robert follows here with a song akin to a suicide note, or one that evokes a clear expectation of death. The bodiless voice cries out as if entangled in the discordant guitar strings, the words weave images of sheer despair, the drunken song staggers deliriously downward to a dark spot where trees are trembling, as the frightened voice imagines to the end that a woman will come and save him from all of this. The spiritual instinct of ancient man is vitally evident here in its grotesque modern guise. The tortured performance is inimitable, with just a couple of "Hellhound" recordings made by others since the original was released. John Shines has told the author, however, that Robert rehearsed the piece so thoroughly that he performed it the same way everywhere he went. There is something awesome about this song. Found on Columbia CL 1654.

(214)

1. Robert prepared his song arrangements so carefully that, unlike most black songsters (see note 60:1) of the day, his performances of individual songs hardly differed.

2. "Terraplane Blues" (see note 171:1) was Robert Johnson's best-selling record.

(216)

1. This incident actually occurred outside a backwoods café, according to John Shines. Calvin Frazier was wanted by the police for this shooting, so he and his companions fled Mississippi and went northward on the lam for several weeks.

(218)

1. See note 96:2.

244

(220)

1. An incident in Robert's travels reported by John Shines as having transpired in Hughes, Arkansas, in 1937. As Shines had it, Robert and the tiny woman proceeded to have an affair.

(221–222)

1. "Bunk's Place" and "Whitechild's" were two of the many roadside clubs and cafes that Robert might have encountered on the road. The ones shown here, including Charley Moleman's (see below), did exist, being familiar to both Houston Stackhouse and John Shines.

(224)

1. John Shines and Mack McCormick have reported that Robert Johnson formed a combo that might have looked something like this; only the electric pickup on the guitar is questionable. Curiously, Robert was listening to a lot of Bing Crosby's recordings after leaving Texas, and was known to perform such numbers as "My Blue Heaven" and "Yes, Sir, That's My Baby" with his band.

(225–226)

1. This incident actually occurred, according to John Shines. Shines noted that it was the only time he ever saw Robert get emotional, let alone cry. And he had never known Robert to play harmonica before, nor did he know that Robert could tap dance. The desperate performance was so successful that the two young men and Calvin Frazier had money enough to buy new guitars.

(227)

1. By 1938, Mississippi's once vigorous lumber industry had fallen into decline, the state's vast woodlands depleted or rendered bare. Federal Writers' Project, op. cit., p. 109.

(228)

1. "I was born around Shaw, Mississippi," recollects David "Honeyboy" Edwards. "That's on 61 highway betwixt Cleveland and Leland. I was raised around Greenwood. We'd go over and stay around Greenwood, come back and stay around Shaw. When I first started to playing I was around fourteen. In probably five or six months I thought I could play: I could play one tune and sing a hundred songs." When David Edwards began to play around the

Delta as a semiprofessional, Charley Patton was still widely respected but living out his last years. Honeyboy heard him and learned some of his signature pieces, including "Pony Blues." He also heard and learned from Robert Johnson, who impressed his contemporaries for breaking away from certain Delta musical practices. But Edwards' principal influences were Tommy McClennan and Robert Petway, who played their dark, droning style of song whenever they came around Greenwood. He was first recorded by Alan Lomax for the Library of Congress in 1942, with this "Worried Life Blues" found on AFS L59. After twenty-five years on the road as an itinerant musician, Honeyboy Edwards settled in Chicago in 1955, where he continues to live and perform today. Robert Palmer, *David "Honeboy" Edwards, Mississippi Delta Bluesman* (New York: Folkways Records, FS 3539), notes.

2. See notes 4:6 and 200:1.

3. A *getback* is a country party or dance, also known as a *frolic*.

4. *Graphonola* was a widespread term in the Afro-American Delta parlance for "record player." It was derived originally from popular trade names Graphophone and Victrola.

5. Itta Bena is a small town south of Greenwood, Mississippi, that attracted many itinerant black musicians in the 1930s. See note 3:1.

6. Three Forks was once a tiny community in the woods between Greenwood and Itta Bena, and today is nothing but an intersection of highways 49E and 82.

(230)

1. A Robert Johnson song about the life of a committed wanderer, the images simple and beautiful, found on Columbia C 30034.

(232)

1. "Little Queen of Spades" is a celebrated Robert Johnson song of modest melodic inspiration that is filled with lyrical funk. The emotional vocal delivery colors the raunchy images perfectly. The line "Everybody say she got a mojo, 'cause she been usin' that stuff," is a reference to the backwoods brand of Afro-American voodoo (see Scene 33 and note 33:1). Found on Columbia C 30034 and Roots RL-339 in different takes.

246

(235)

1. Robert Johnson's "From Four Till Late" takes its aged melody from "The Four O'Clock Blues," one of the earliest of blues songs. Its reference to Gulfport, Mississippi, creates the possibility that Robert first learned it from Ike Zinnerman (see note 22:2) down around Hazlehurst. It seems to have its imaginal origins in the Eastern seaboard blues traditions, and Robert's version does mention Norfolk, the Virginia harbor town. Found on Columbia C 30034.

(237–238)

1. "Stop Breakin' Down Blues" is a unique, twelve-bar blues by Robert that despite its narrative form is actually a fast-paced dance piece. The Rolling Stones recorded a high-water version on their "Exile on Main Street" LP, and the original release can be found on Columbia C 30034, but the outtake available on Roots RL-339 is best of all.

(239)

1. Honeyboy Edwards remembers being with Robert Johnson on this fateful night. When he left the party early, too drunk to go on, he was unaware of Robert's poisoning.

2. "Milkcow's Calf Blues" is the last song Robert Johnson recorded. It was taken from Kokomo Arnold's popular "Milk Cow Blues," and contains a line from the 1930 Son House recording, "My Black Mama." Robert's emotionally urgent version was a crowd pleaser. The western swing band, Cliff Bruner's Texas Wanderers, playfully salutes Robert by imitating his vocal style in a verse from their own "Milk Cow Blues." Found on Columbia CL 1654.

(240)

1. "Phonograph Blues" is a Robert Johnson song bearing more sexual images and metaphors. Two unusually distinct versions are to be found on Columbia C 30034 and Roots RL-339.

2. Controversy has long enshrouded the death of Robert Johnson. For many years following the murder, scores of rumors in the black community even made the death itself uncertain. As for the cause of death, these rumors generally supposed that a stabbing by some jealous woman was most likely. Over the last decade, however, Mack McCormick has gathered enough evidence—an interview with the murderer included—to conclude reasonably that Robert Johnson was poisoned by a jealous man, as these scenes have imagined.

3. As it was envisaged cinematically, this scene is not complete without the added element of a particular Ethiopian tribal music, a *fila* flute dance. The recording of this trance piece, which is performed by two circles of flute players dancing and chanting in opposite rotations, induces a dark ancestral awareness in the listener that lends the total image a hallucinatory character. Found on the Ocora (Office de Radiodiffusion-Television Française) LP, *Musiques Éthiopiennes*, OCR 75.

(242)

1. Events proceeded in a peculiar manner after Robert's poisoning. He did not die right away, says Mack McCormick, but was taken away in a feeble state by a black man whom no one has ever been able to identify. Our understanding of his name is a phonetic one, and McCormick is not sure if the name is properly pronounced "Tush Hogg" or "Tushogg." In any case, this mysterious fellow took Robert to a little shack and put him to bed, watching over him for three days. When Robert Johnson finally died he had not yet seen a doctor, so one wonders who this stranger "Tush Hogg" was and why he let Robert die. To make matters worse, McCormick discovered a death certificate signed by Jim Moore, whose identity is also unknown. Maybe Moore drove a white pickup truck.

2. Robert Johnson's family insists that Robert turned his soul over to Jesus Christ just before he died. Robert's half-sister claims to have obtained a slip of linen paper bearing Robert's last words, which confirm this deathbed conversion. The authenticity of the conversion and its written "proof" is doubtful, the meaningfulness of it all negligible, unless placed within the context of myth.

(243)

1. Washington Phillips was born in Freestone County, Texas, around the year 1891. His father Houston Phillips and mother Emma Titas were both native Texans. Between 1927 and 1929, Washington Phillips recorded eighteen songs for a field unit of Columbia Records, which was doing all the gospel recording it would do before the Depression. By recording Blind Willie Johnson at the same time as Phillips, these field units produced the most important Afro-American religious music ever documented on disk (see note 2:2). Phillips' incomparable recordings seem to have been quite successful commercially. Part of his success may be attrib-

utable to his weird sound. He accompanied himself on a *dulceola,* about which an acquaintance of Phillips named Frank Walker has said, "Nobody on earth could use it except him—nobody would want to, I don't think." It was related to the hammered dulcimer, and created a heavenly, childlike sound unlike any instrument anywhere. Beyond this, Phillips was a genuine singer and a fascinating one. About half of his songs on record are traditional, the rest he composed himself, and all of them reflect a common, simple folk morality quite suspicious of the ways of the modern, urbanized world. Phillips ended his short career with "I Had a Good Father and Mother," a song of breathtaking innocence and grace. Very few copies of this record were sold because it was released in the depths of the Depression. With his occupation listed as "farmer," an Austin State Hospital death certificate reveals that Washington Phillips died December 31, 1938, of pulmonary tuberculosis. Since Austin State Hospital was an insane asylum, and since Phillips was treated there for eight years, one month and four days before he died, it is improbable that TB was the main reason for his hospitalization. The fact that the death certificate lists his wife as "unknown" supports this supposition, because families commonly put their mentally deranged away and forgot about them, until recently. Among Washington Phillips' unforgettable recordings are "Take Your Burden to the Lord and Leave It There," "A Mother's Last Word to Her Daughter," "A Mother's Last Word to Her Son" and "Denomination Blues, Parts 1 and 2." Guido van Rijn and Hans Vergeer, *Washington Phillips/"Denomination Blues"* (Ter Aar, The Netherlands: Agram Records, Blues AB-2006), liner notes.

2. Towards the end of 1938 John Hammond began lining up performers for his "From Spirituals to Swing" concert. Having heard the ARC recordings of Robert Johnson released on the Vocalion label, Hammond telephoned Don Law in Dallas and asked him to track down the mercurial young singer and get him to Carnegie Hall somehow. Law was doubtful that Robert could handle the atmosphere and audience, but notified Ernie Oertle nevertheless. It was Oertle who went to Mississippi and sent back the first word of Robert Johnson's death. It might be added that the murder went unreported until 1974, when historian Mack McCormick informed the Greenwood police.

3. Robert Johnson was buried in a pinewood coffin furnished by the county, the grave site as yet undetermined. One report has his grave located beside the Little Zion Church near Greenwood. Robert's mother and brother-in-law attended his burial.

Selected Discography

ANTHOLOGIES

Aolt Records 101. *Light Crust Doughboys, Vol. 1*, produced by Ray Doggett.

Arhoolie Records: Old Timey LP 116. *Western Swing, Vol. 2* (Jimmie Revard, Milton Brown, Light Crust Doughboys, Adolph Hofner, W. Lee O'Daniel, Washboard Wonders, Bob Wills), edited by Chris Strachwitz.

BC LP No. 19. *Negro Religious Music, Vol. 3: Singing Preachers and Their Congregations* (Rev. D. C. Rice, Rev. F. McGhee, Elder Otis Jones, Elder Lightfoot Solomon Michaux, Rev. Kelsey, Rev. C. C. Chapman), edited by Chris Strachwitz.

Biograph BLP-12027. *This Old World's in a Hell of a Fix* (The Gospel according to Skip James, Fred McDowell, Robert Wilkins, Black Billy Sunday, Jaybird Coleman, Washington Phillips).

Ethnic Folkways Library FE 4417. *Negro Folk Music of Alabama —Secular* (recorded in Alabama by Harold Courlander).

Folklyric Records 9004. *Corridos, Part 1: 1930–1934* (Hermanos Bañuelos, Pedro Rocha & Lupe Martinez, Nacho & Justino, Hermanos Sanchez & Linares), edited by Chris Strachwitz.

Folkways Records FJ-2807. *Jazz New York: 1922–34* (Louis Armstrong, Jack Teagarden, Duke Ellington, Fletcher Henderson, Fats Waller, Louisiana Rhythm Kings).

Folkways Records FS 3841. *See Island Folk Festival* (Moving Star Hall Singers and Alan Lomax).

Historical Records, Melodeon MLP 7324. *Party Blues* (Tampa Red's Hokum Jug Band, Red Nelson, Bo Carter, Blind Blake, John Hurt, Memphis Jug Band).

Library of Congress, Music Division, Recording Laboratory, AFS L67. *Afro-American Folk Music from Tate and Panola Counties,*

Mississippi (from the Archive of American Folk Song), edited by David Evans.

Library of Congress, Music Division, Recording Laboratory, AAFS L10. *Folk Music of the United States: Negro Religious Songs and Services* (from the Archive of American Folk Song), edited by B. A. Botkin.

Library of Congress, Music Division, Recording Laboratory, AAFS L3. *Folk Music of the United States: Afro-American Spirituals, Work Songs, and Ballads* (from the Archive of American Folk Song), edited by Alan Lomax.

Library of Congress, Music Division, Recording Laboratory, AFS L4. *Folk Music of the United States: Afro-American Blues and Game Songs* (from the Archive of American Folk Song), edited by Alan Lomax.

New World Records NW-252. *Roots of the Blues* (Lining Hymn and Prayer, Church-House Moan, Field Song from Senegal).

Ocora Records OCR 75. *Musiques Éthiopiennes* (Office de Radiodiffusion-Television Française), directed by Charles Duvelle.

Ocora Records 558511. *Burundi: Musiques Traditionnelles,* with the cooperation of the Voice of the Revolution of Burundi, OCR 40.

Origin OJL-5. *The Mississippi Blues 1927–1940* (John Hurt, Bukka White, Willie Brown, Son House, William Harris).

Origin OJL-13. *In the Spirit, Vol. 2* (Mother McCollum, Blind Willie Johnson, Washington Phillips, Charley Patton).

RBF Records RBF-14. *Blues Roots: Mississippi* (Tommy Johnson, Bo Carter, Joe Williams, Robert Johnson, Tommy McClennan, Robert Petway, Mississippi Jook Band).

Riverside Records SDP-II. *History of Classic Jazz* (Rev. J. M. Gates, Blind Lemon Jefferson, Street Cries of Charleston-1926, Ida Cox, Chippie Hill, Georgia Camp Meeting, Cripple Clarence Lofton).

Roots RL-339. *Delta Blues* (Robert Johnson, Skip James, Son House, Charley Patton), Limited Edition.

Roots Special Edition RSE-5. *Legendary Sessions, Delta Style* (Willie Brown, Son House, Louise Johnson), Collectors' Series.

Roots RL-314. *Mississippi Blues, Vol. 3* (Poor Boy Lofton's "Jake Leg Blues," Robert Johnson, John Hurt, Robert Petway, Bo Carter, Mississippi Sheiks, Tommy McClennan), Limited Edition.

Rounder Records 2014. *Get Your Ass in the Water and Swim Like Me!* (*Narrative Poetry from Black Oral Tradition*), recorded and edited by Bruce Jackson.

Stash ST-101. *Copulatin' Blues—Vol. 1* (Sidney Bechet, Lil Johnson, Bessie Smith, Coot Grant, Tampa Red's Hokum Band, Jelly Roll Morton, Lucille Bogan).

Yazoo Records L-1004. *Tex-Arkana-Louisiana Country 1929–1933* (Buddy Boy Hawkins, Henry Thomas, Texas Alexander, King Solomon Hill), edited by Stephen Calt.

INDIVIDUAL ARTISTS

Ellington, Duke.
In Hollywood/On the Air 1933–40, Members of the Duke Ellington Society, Max Records MLP-1001, Limited Edition.

House, Son.
The Legendary 1941–1942 Recordings in Chronological Sequence (incl. Willie Brown, Fiddlin' Joe Martin), Folklyric 9002.

James, Skip.
King of the Delta Blues Singers. Biograph BLP-12029.

Johnson, Blind Willie.
Blind Willie Johnson 1927–1930, RBF Records RBF-10.

———.
Blind Willie Johnson, His Story Told, Annotated and Documented by Samuel B. Charters, Folkways Records FG-3585.

Johnson, Lonnie.
Mr. Johnson's Blues 1926–1932, Mamlish Records S-3807.

Johnson, Robert.
King of the Delta Blues Singers (Vol. 1), Thesaurus of Classic Jazz, Columbia CL 1654.

———.
King of the Delta Blues Singers (Vol. 2), Columbia C 30034.

Johnson, Tommy.
The Famous 1928 Tommy Johnson-Ishman Bracey Session, Roots RL-330.

Owens, Jack.
Mississippi Country Blues (with Bud Spires), Testament Records T-2222.

Patton, Charley.
Charley Patton, Founder of the Delta Blues, Yazoo L-1020.

Patton, Charley.
Patton, Sims, and Bertha Lee—Bottleneck Guitar Pioneer, Herwin Records 213.

Phillips, Washington.
Denomination Blues, Agram Records, Blues AB-2006.

Thomas, Henry.
Ragtime Texas—Complete Recorded Works, 1927–1929, Herwin Records 209, notes by Mack McCormick.

Wilkins, Rev. Robert.
Memphis Gospel Singer (including "Prodigal Son"), Music Research, Inc., Piedmont Records PLP-13162.